A Mountain
On My Back
MEMOIR OF A CHINESE WOMAN

Youfeng Shen

Contents

Acknowledgments

It takes a village to raise a child. As it turns out, it took a whole village to complete this book. I would like to express my appreciation to my family and friends all over the world that have participated and cheered me on during this 10 year journey. I have realized that writing a book is harder than I thought but more rewarding than I could have ever imagined.

This book would have been impossible if not for the constant support and encouragement of my friend, editor and mentor, Joy Fisher, who is always there for me when I have questions and need her advice. Aloha, Joy, on the blue-sky, beautiful Big Island!

I started to write this book about 10 years ago. But when my husband got cancer, I had to stop everything to care for him. Thank God he recovered and is now in remission for the past eight years. During this on-and-off journey, my husband has always been very supportive and was always the first reader of each chapter.

I would also like to thank my family, the Shen family: my daughter, brothers and sisters, who have generously allowed me to tell their stories. They wrote me emails and messages, providing me with accounts about themselves and about our family. My daughter, though always too busy like most grown children, understood the importance of this book to me and took the time to closely read everything and helped me shape the overall structure of the book, supplementing facts and sentiments throughout the book with her own memories. Along the way, we discussed, argued, laughed, cried, and remembered, as a family does.

I am also extremely fortunate to have my husband's sisters who are willing to be my readers and give me valuable feedback and suggestions. Thank you, Ann, Nelle and Jean! I am grateful for Nelle's support as she had previous publishing experience in Canada and was so efficient in editing my final draft and helping me across the finishing line.

Last, but not least, I would like to extend my gratitude to all my friends and colleagues who assisted me in various ways: Suzanne Fox from Carson City, Nevada; Dorothy Chikasawa from Davis, California; Dr. Amy Matthewson from London, England and Betsy Collins and Diana Lee Vriend from Sacramento, California.

I am dedicating this book posthumously to the most loving and inspirational couple I have ever known, Jack and Valerie Bass. They have touched me and so many others in so many ways. Their talents and compassion in music, their love and support for family and friends, especially their volunteer work and service for the local communities and the United Nations will always be remembered. They will live forever in my heart and the hearts of many others who knew them.

Prologue
SEPTEMBER 20, 1989

"Look, Xiao Bo, you just fold three sheets of toilet paper lengthwise like this and insert both ends into the straps on this menstrual belt. This way the toilet paper stays in place on the belt. Then you wear it inside your underwear."

My hands expertly folded the paper padding as I tried to show my 12-year-old daughter how to prepare for her first menstrual cycle. The toilet paper used in China at that time was about the size of printer paper and made of a white, rough, and porous material. It had to be prepared carefully to absorb menstrual flow as effectively as possible and reduce chafing. Before my impending departure to America, I felt compelled to prepare Xiao Bo for this important rite of passage in becoming a woman, just as my mother had done for me. There was a high likelihood that her time would come while I could not be by her side.

Xiao Bo nodded, and, when asked, repeated the procedure a couple of times to show that she had retained the steps. I knew that when the time actually came, there would be more questions, but this was the best I could do for now.

As we put the demonstration materials away, Xiao Bo touched my hand and looked up at me with her dark, quiet eyes, "Mama, why do you have to leave?"

My voice choked a little when I tried to answer. I waited for it to pass and put my arms around her, "Remember what we talked about before? Mama is going to America to study and find a job. It should just be for two years. And then I will bring you, Grandma and Grandpa to America. We will all have a better life there together. I promise."

Xiao Bo clung to my arm and kept looking at me in her quiet way. I saw behind her eyes the questions she swallowed and did not ask as her young mind struggled to understand and accept what she could not change. Finally, she relaxed into my arms and said, "Yes, Mama, I understand you are doing this for both of us and for Grandma and Grandpa." My heart ached with pride, sadness, and hope.

The day of departure came. September 20th, 1989 was a beautiful autumn day, but my heart was filled with sadness and apprehension. It was the most painful and difficult decision I had ever made —to leave my only child, my family and my homeland behind. Xiao Bo held onto my hand tightly the entire way to the airport. I was not sure I could go through with it if I even glanced at her one more time. It ripped my heart apart just imagining we would be separated for two years while I searched for a better life in America. My brothers and sisters smiled at me encouragingly while tears glistened in their eyes. Summoning all my determination and courage, I boarded the Air China flight bound for San Francisco. I did not look back. I was leaving behind everything I cherished: my 12-year-old daughter, my beloved and aging parents, my five loving and supportive siblings and my stable teaching position. I had with me only my passport, a full two-year scholarship to the University of

Cincinnati in Ohio, two suitcases filled with only necessary books and clothes and my dreams of freedom in America.

Even though I had promised Professor Zhang, the dean of the English Department, that in two years I would return to teach at the Shanghai University, I had made up my mind to leave China for good. I was seeking better opportunities for my daughter, my family and myself, and I hoped to provide a more comfortable life for my aging parents during their retirement years.

I had no idea what awaited me in America. I knew little about America except what came to me through letters and word of mouth from friends and former students now living in America. As I plunged into the great unknown, I had some doubt and fear about my inability to overcome all obstacles. But I was determined to focus all my energy to find a way to conquer all difficulties and face the new challenges in front of me.

As the plane lifted off, I considered the circuitous chain of events that had led me to this painful and difficult decision, a decision which would change the course of my life and my daughter's life forever.

Youfeng Shen

1 – Family Roots
1948-1956

I was born into the Shen family on November 2, 1948, the year of the Rat. My parents named me Youfeng, which means "Having Phoenix". In Chinese mythology the phoenix is a symbol of heaven's favor, virtue and grace, and it is also the female counterpart to the dragon. Unrelated to the auspicious bird that we know in the western world that rises from the ashes and symbolizes rebirth, the Chinese phoenix symbolizes peace and prosperity.

I entered the world five months before the end of our long civil war between the Guomindang (The Chinese Nationalist Party) and the Communist Party. When Mao Zedong's armies swept across the Yangtze River in mid-April 1949, the capital city of Nanjing surrendered without a fight, as did the cities and towns along the road to Shanghai. At midnight on April 24, 1949, General Chen Yi's peasant soldiers entered Shanghai. When the city awoke the next day, it found itself under new management of the Chinese Communist Party. On October 1, 1949, the People's Republic of China was officially established in Beijing, and by the end of that year, Chiang Kai-Shek and roughly two million Guomindang personnel had completely withdrawn from the mainland to the island of Taiwan about 100 miles offshore.

My life began at this point in modern Chinese history when the weary and war-ridden Chinese people were eager to settle down to a simple, peaceful life after four decades of war.

When I was growing up, I was constantly made aware by my parents that as one of the oldest children I was expected to set a good example for my younger brothers and sisters. As the eldest daughter, I was also expected to do my best to win honor for my parents and my whole family. Had I done less, I would have felt very guilty. My parents' approval was my primary concern. It was a basic Chinese concept of filial piety that children must respect elders and behave properly and responsibly in all things. Otherwise you would bring disgrace not only upon yourself but, more importantly, upon everyone in your family, especially your parents and ancestors. We believed that both living and deceased relatives were "watching you" at all times. As a good daughter, I always felt that I carried a mountain on my back because I had the responsibility for the well-being and honor of my family.

My family lived in a mixed Shanghai neighborhood of factory workers, shopkeepers and teachers. Our lane was named Hai Xin Guang Li (Starlight of the Ocean) and was located off South Town Street, a small side street behind Xuhui Middle School. This school served the Xuhui District and faced a main boulevard. Our house was in a complex of one- and two-storey houses facing each other in two rows of twelve houses each. Between the houses was a rectangular yard 30 feet wide and about 200 feet deep. This large enclosed courtyard was our main activity area or playground.

The houses were constructed of red and gray bricks with black tile roofs. The wooden front doors were painted dark red or brown. Each door had a house number on the top, usually followed by a Chinese character posted for good luck, health and prosperity. Most of the homes had a small backyard where some families raised ducks and chickens. Some yards still contained old concrete-rimmed wells which had been used prior to the installation of several common water taps in the courtyard. Many of these wells, including ours, had been filled in with earth to prevent animals and small children from falling into them. Homes in our neighborhood did not have running water, indoor plumbing or gas until the early 1980's. Our family toilet, a movable wooden chamber-pot with a handle and a lid, was placed in a small shed in a corner of our backyard. There was also a small chamber pot in the attic where my mother and most of the children slept. Both had to be emptied and cleaned daily.

When I was young, all housing was assigned by the local neighborhood committee. Assignments were based on family size and employment status. The local neighborhood committee was usually composed of a Communist Party secretary, who chaired the committee, several representatives of the local residents and a local police department representative.

Because of the growing population and limited housing, two families usually shared one house. Mr. and Mrs. Cheng and their adopted daughter, Meili, shared the house with us. They were like an extended family and everyone knew everyone else's business. Privacy was a luxury very few could afford. We knew exactly what the Chengs ate for dinner and how much income they had, and they knew the same about us. The Chengs occupied the two rooms at the front of the house. They used the front one as a combined kitchen, living and dining room and the second one as a separate bedroom.

Our family of eight occupied the third room at the back of the house and the entire attic. We used the downstairs room as a combined kitchen and living area. It contained a square kitchen table surrounded by two long benches and some chairs. This table was the most used piece of furniture in our home. There, our family prepared and ate meals and gathered to socialize and talk. Most of the time, all six children did their homework on this table after school. The remaining space in the kitchen was filled by a bamboo-framed bed, an old wicker chair, a big water container behind the door and several small bamboo stools.

Access to the attic was by a 30-inch wide wooden ladder located in the common hallway that ran along one side of the house. This ladder was hinged to the wall. To go upstairs, we simply unhooked the ladder, swung it out from the wall and locked it in place. Then we climbed up through a trap door in the floor of the attic loft. There, a single large bedroom ran the entire 36-foot length of the house. The only furniture in the attic included one queen-sized bamboo bed, one full-sized wooden bed and a five-drawer bureau where we kept all our sheets, blankets and pillow cases.

There was a big double window in the attic facing south. Whenever there was sunshine, we placed our bedding and quilts on the sun-warmed roof tiles just outside the window to air out. We dried our main wash downstairs on movable bamboo rods hanging from the front of our house. A smaller, north-facing window about five feet above the floor opposite the big south window gave us light as well as a welcome cross-breeze on hot summer days. The attic ceiling sloped; the lowest point was on either side, about waist-high from the floor. Along this space, we stored our boxes full of the family's winter or summer clothes, depending on the season.

Our father usually slept downstairs with my elder brother. My mother usually slept in the queen-sized bed in the middle of the big attic room with the current baby (the youngest child) and one or two girls at her feet. But when she was in the last month of pregnancy and could no longer safely climb up the ladder, she would sleep downstairs. Then my elder brother would sleep on the floor in the attic.

I remember vividly how my elder brother Youfu (Having Good Fortune) and I decided to prepare the family breakfast one cold spring morning when I was about six years old. I was awakened by the noise of our hen clucking in the yard below. I was in our big bed, still holding onto my mother's big toe. "The hen must have delivered another egg," I thought. I awakened slowly, a little at a time, and realized Mother was still in bed. My younger brother Yougen (Having Roots), who was about two years old, lay peacefully in her arms. I climbed out of bed very carefully and tiptoed to Mother's side to check on her.

My mother heard me and said, her eyes still closed, "Youfeng, wake up your elder brother and tell him to get ready for school."

"Yes, Mama," I replied, wondering why she was still in bed. She was usually downstairs by now cooking breakfast. "Are you all right, Mama?" I asked as I looked at her puffed, pale face next to my younger brother's fat, pink, apple-shaped face.

"I'm all right, just a little dizzy this morning," Mother said, her eyes still closed.

Dad had left early for the morning shift at the textile factory. Mama was about seven months pregnant with her fourth child. I noticed that lately she had been having dizzy spells more frequently than usual. I went downstairs and saw my elder brother still sleeping soundly. I shook his shoulder and said, "Gege (elder brother) wake up. Gege, wake up!"

Youfu woke up suddenly and asked: "Wha-wha-what's wrong, M-m-Meimei (younger sister)? Is-is M-m-Mama O-o-Ok?" Youfu stuttered until he went to middle school. He started out imitating a classmate who stuttered and then he caught it too.

Youfu jumped out of bed. "I-i-is the-there so-some th-thing wro-wrong? I-is M-m-Mama h-h-ha-having a-a b-ba-baby?" I laughed at him and said:

"Nothing is wrong, Gege. Mama is just dizzy."

Youfu quickly put on his clothes. He was about eight years old and was in the first grade, but he nevertheless took charge of the situation.

"I-I-th-think-w-we sh-should-s-start th-the f-fire t-to co-co-cook b-bre-break-k-fast f-fo-for M-m-Mama."

He put on his shoes quickly and started to wrestle the empty iron stove out of the house into the backyard. The stove was pretty heavy, but Youfu managed to maneuver it outside by himself.

Meanwhile, I found our hen's egg, which was still warm, lying in a straw nest in the shade. Before I carefully carried it inside, I grabbed some uncooked rice and fed it to the hen. She was still clucking happily, proudly reporting her new egg. I put the egg in a small bowl and helped my brother collect some old newspapers and kindling to start a fire as we had seen our mother do so many times before.

After we lit the fire and the kindling began to burn, we added some small pieces of wood and placed a cylindrical brick of coal on top of the wood. The coal would burn all day long in our stove and was our only source for both warmth and cooking. Youfu and I took turns fanning the fire until the wood smoke disappeared and the coal was glowing red. The stove was too hot for Youfu to lift alone, so we found kitchen towels to protect our hands, picked it up by its handles, and carried it back inside the house.

Mama must have heard us in the kitchen because she was climbing downstairs slowly, one foot at a time. She was swollen all over, like a big balloon. Whenever I touched her hands or feet it would leave deep indentations in her skin. When she saw us carrying the stove inside the house, she could not believe that we had already lit the stove.

"I was thinking about getting some soybean milk from the store for breakfast, but now we don't have to spend the money. We can cook porridge instead," she said as she slowly sat down in the old wicker chair by the kitchen table.

"I know how to cook porridge, Mama," I volunteered. "It's easy. You just pour some hot water onto leftover rice and cook it until it's boiling." Eager to please my mother, I reached out my right arm, trying to grab the thermos bottle, but the wall shelf was too high for me.

"N-no-no, le-le-let m-m-me do-do i-it. Yo-you-you a-a-are t-to-too sh-sh-short!" my elder brother shouted. I stopped my hand in midair.

"Neither of you should touch the thermos bottle yet. I am glad you children lit the stove and brought it inside, but it's dangerous. Next time, let me bring it inside." Mother warned us and continued, "You can put two ladles of cold water into the rice pot. It just takes a little longer for the rice to boil."

Following her instructions, I scooped two ladles of water from a big container behind the door and poured the water into the rice pot. Then Youfu set the rice pot on the stove. In about 15 to 20 minutes, the porridge was ready, and the three of us sat down to a nice hot bowl of porridge with pickles and fermented Sichuan tofu. (This is the Chinese equivalent of an American breakfast of hot oatmeal with raisins and milk.)

After that day it became Youfu's regular job to light the stove each morning. Dad would take the stove outside to the backyard before he left for work, and Mama would bring it back into the kitchen after the fire stopped smoking. My job was to sweep the cement floor in the kitchen area and feed the hen. Everyone in the family had a list of daily household chores, and no one ever complained. My family worked as a team to get through each day. It became a matter of course to increase our chores and responsibilities as we grew older.

Just before our mother's due date, our maternal grandma traveled by train from Shaoxing, our family's hometown, to Shanghai in early May 1955. Shaoxing is about 120 miles southeast of Shanghai. My grandma was born there in 1901. Her first name was Xinghua (Apricot Blossom) since she had a beautiful oval face with soft, fair skin. She was in her late 50s, but she still had her long, soft black hair coiled into a tight bun on the back of her head. She always wore dark blue or gray clothes and a pair of small, pointed black shoes because her feet had been bound when she was very young.

When my grandma came to visit, she would tell us stories. This is the story she told us about her feet: When she was about five, her mother had broken her toes and started to bind her feet with traditional 10-foot-long cloth strips to keep her feet from growing. The practice of foot binding originated among upper class court dancers in the 10th century in China, then became popular and spread to all social classes by the Qing dynasty. The ideal length of the bound feet was three Chinese inches (about four inches in Western measurement) and the tight bindings were applied to modify the shape and length to resemble the "three-inch golden lotus." Normal-sized feet were considered ugly and bound feet were considered erotic at that time in Chinese culture. They were also regarded as the mark of a virtuous woman.

Grandma remembered crying all day and all night from the constant, burning pain in her feet. She said that every time her feet touched the floor, the pain felt as if her whole body were on fire. She begged her mother to unbind her feet, but her mother always said, "Xinghua, I know it's painful. But in order for you to marry into a good family, you need to suffer just like I did when I was your age. It's for the sake of your future."

The only time my grandma could get a little relief from the excruciating pain was when her mother let her wash her feet. She remembered the horrible smell from her feet whenever she opened the bindings. In summertime, when her toes swelled up and filled with pus, her father had to find some herbal medicines to relieve her pain and swelling. She could not walk properly for a couple of years.

She turned 11 the year after Dr. Sun Yatsen, the founder of the Guomindang government, banned this cruel practice in 1911. Her feet were released from her bindings eventually, leaving a permanent but less severe deformity than what many women of previous generations had suffered. My grandma's feet were about five inches long.

My grandma told me that she was fortunate that Dr. Sun Yatsen had banned this cruel custom. In some remote mountain areas of China, women were still having their feet bound until 1949, when the People's Republic of China finally outlawed this barbaric practice.

Shaoxing was the hometown where my parents grew up and where our family had lived for many generations. When my parents got married in 1941, Japanese soldiers were still invading China. They had a reputation for raping any young women they found unprotected. To protect my mother on the journey to her wedding, my grandma traveled the 120 miles from Shaoxing to Shanghai with her 20-year-old daughter. Shanghai was where my father worked as a dye-master. It was an arranged marriage between the two families. My parents were married as soon as my mother arrived in Shanghai.

Over the years, my mother bore 10 children, four of whom died at birth or during the first few months of life. Every time Mother had a baby, my grandma made the 120-mile trip to Shanghai and stayed with us for a couple of months to help with my mother's recovery. After giving birth, most Chinese women were expected to rest in bed and do nothing for one month. Grandma's job was to help our mother take care of the new-born baby and everything in the house while our mother rested and recovered.

Grandma would often tell us about Shaoxing and its rich fields, beautiful rivers, canals and mountains. She also told us about her father, who had been a scholar in Shaoxing. My maternal great-grandfather used to conduct a private school in his home. As a young girl, my grandma would hide in the next room, and then come out peeping through a screen to listen to her father's lectures. She heard her father reciting Dao De Jing by Lao Zi with his students.

Lao Zi was a philosopher who lived around 500 BC. He is best known for Dao De Jing (The Book of the Way and Its Virtue) which is one of the most translated books in history, alongside the Bible and the Quran. The very first line of the Dao De Jing says, "The Dao that can be told is not the eternal Dao." Here, the Dao means the way, the path of the universe. One of the most important principles of Daoism is living a simple and balanced life in harmony with nature.

At first, my grandma could not understand what her father was teaching, but she memorized many of his teachings while listening behind the screen. When her father discovered that she was eavesdropping from behind the screen and wanted to learn, he let her sit in a chair in the corner but asked her to keep quiet. In his late 50s, my great-grandfather became very ill and closed his school. During the last few months of his life, he had become demented, writing letters to heaven and burning them as some kind of offerings. My grandma was only 17 when her father died in the winter of 1918.

Two years later my grandma and grandfather were married. As was customary, the marriage was arranged between the two families by a local matchmaker. My grandfather was 31 and my grandma was only 19. It was considered good luck for a woman to marry an older man, because it was felt that a husband who was some years senior to his wife would cherish his wife and his children more after having waited and saved for so long to get married.

But my grandma was not that lucky. My grandfather turned out to be a weak, selfish, and lazy man. He was from a rich family and indulged himself in teahouses playing mahjong all day long and never worked a single day in his life. They were living a pretty comfortable life at the time of their marriage, but my grandfather eventually managed to lose their money and property at the mahjong tables. As a result, my grandparents ended up living in a townhouse that my maternal great-grandfather had left to my grandma when he died. My grandparents continued living in that house until my grandfather's death in 1965. My grandma stayed on there until her own death in 1982.

My grandma had four children. My mother was the eldest daughter in the Tan family. Her given name was Aiding (Love of Tranquility). In 1929, when my mother was only eight years old, she was sent by her father to live and work as an apprentice in an embroidery shop in Hangzhou, about 40 miles from Shaoxing. My grandma wanted him to stop his gambling, but she was powerless to make him do so. Women were supposed to obey their fathers when they were young, obey their husbands when they were married and obey their sons when widowed. That was the traditional Chinese way of life.

My mother's life as a child apprentice was sheer drudgery. There were no child labor regulations at that time. My mother was essentially treated as an indentured servant and was rousted out of bed by her master as soon as the rooster crowed at dawn. She had to start the fire in the family stove, and heat a large pot of water for her master's whole family to use. She assisted two other older girls who had finished their apprenticeships already. After breakfast she cleaned the dishes, swept the dirt floor in the kitchen and mopped the wooden floor in the working area. When it was bright enough to see the needles and patterns, she sat down and started embroidering with the others.

She was trained by her master's wife and she learned very quickly. Usually she would sit still embroidering all morning until it was time for a short lunch break. Lunch consisted of a bowl of rice with pickles or sometimes salted fish and a cup of tea. After lunch, she would resume her work until it was too dark to see. She started out embroidering tablecloths and pillowcases. As her skills improved, she was given more complex tasks such as bedcovers, lady's clothing and sometimes even wedding dresses. After dinner, she was expected to clean the table and wash dishes by candlelight. She worked continuously for more than 12 hours a day. She was a virtual slave to her master, and the little money she did earn was sent back home to her father.

My mother had begun to lose her baby teeth just before she left home. Her new teeth came in crooked. Her permanent teeth grew out while her baby teeth were still in place. No adult was around who cared about her enough to check on her or help to remove her baby teeth, so she had a whole mouthful of uneven teeth when she finally saw her mother again two years later.

She was trying to survive under the constant nagging and criticism of her master. He would yell at her, "Aiding, you are taking too long to finish this pillow case." Or, "the stitches of the flowers are not even." One afternoon, she was so tired that she dozed off on top of her embroidery frame. When the master saw her dozing off, he beat her with a bamboo stick on her head, shoulders and arms until his wife begged him to stop. She begged, "Dang jia de (the master of the house), Aiding is still a child, please don't anger yourself. She cannot work for us if you injure her and we have so much work to be done."

My mother often wept silently over her plight at night so as not to awaken her roommates. By the time she was 10 years old, she missed her mother and family so much that she planned to run away and return home. She told a family friend Uncle Li how frequently her master beat her. This Uncle Li was from the same village and worked in a silk factory in Hangzhou not very far from her master's house. He had brought her to this embroidery shop two years before. My mother showed him the bruises on her neck, shoulders and arms. Uncle Li agreed to take her back home to Shaoxing on his next monthly visit to see his wife and children. When that day came, my mother sneaked away before dawn to meet Uncle Li at his factory dormitory, so that no one would notice that she was missing. She had not dared to close her eyes even for a minute that night.

When my grandma saw my mother after two years' separation, she could not believe that this pale, thin waif was her daughter. Her soft round face had become rough and thin. Her teeth looked awful. There were bruises all over her body. Grandma had been unaware that her daughter had been so cruelly treated and abused.

My selfish grandfather wanted to send her back, but for once my grandma stood up to him and defended her daughter.

My mother told her father she would rather die than go back. In the end her father had to let her stay, but he put her to work in the fields growing rice and vegetables. My uncle, who was three years younger than my mother, joined her in the fields, while their father continued his daily routine at the teahouse.

The following year my maternal uncle began to attend the village school nearby in the mornings, so he could only work for half a day. He was the only son in the Tan family; therefore, he received some education. Girls did not have the opportunity to attend any kind of school unless the family was very wealthy.

My mother's two younger sisters began helping in the fields as soon as they were able to carry and use the garden tools. The family kept the rice they grew for themselves but sold most of their vegetables at the market. Sometimes they got cash and sometimes they bartered the vegetables in exchange for other household items. They also made embroidered tablecloths and sewed clothes and shoes during the winter season to sell at the market for extra money. Grandma's stories made me feel closer to her, and at the same time I felt very lucky that I didn't have to go through what my mother had gone through when she was growing up in Shaoxing.

As a little girl, I often wished Grandma would live with us all the time. But she had two other daughters living in different places and she performed the same birthing duties for them as she did for us. She also went to help my uncle and his wife who lived in Suzhou, about 70 miles northwest of Shanghai when her daughter-in-law gave birth.

My grandma traveled a lot in spite of the fact that she had "half-bound" feet. She could walk almost as fast as normal people and could stand a couple of hours on her feet around the house before having to rest them. Every time she washed her feet, I watched her. Carefully taking her feet out of the tiny pointed shoes that she made for herself, she would say with relief, "Merciful Buddha! I don't have to unbind those stinky long cloth strips anymore."

My grandma enjoyed visiting her daughters and spending time with her grandchildren. She functioned like a traveling midwife. She came to Shanghai in May 1955 to help deliver my younger sister and take care of my mother and my family. After three months in Shanghai, she returned home and rested for a couple of months. In November she had to go to my second aunt's home in Hangzhou to help her and her family with a birth. The following March it was her third daughter's turn to have a baby. Luckily her third daughter lived nearby in Shaoxing, so my grandma did not have to travel out of town.

For over 15 years, between 1946 and 1962, my grandma took only brief breaks from this routine because her three daughters and one daughter-in-law produced a total of 23 grandchildren during this period. She was indeed a "super" grandma and a valuable member of the family who we all needed, loved and venerated.

Grandma taught us by example. She was a devout Buddhist and a vegetarian. Although she didn't go to temples often, she lived a special way of life. She got up very early each morning, lighted three sticks of incense and put them in a jar filled with uncooked rice. Then she bowed and started her meditation in front of a small Buddha statue at the far end of our kitchen shelf. She did the same thing again at night before going to bed. Sometimes we could hear her chanting. We kept very quiet whenever we saw her alone in that corner.

One day, I asked her what she was doing and what her chanting was about. She answered, "I am practicing my Buddhist rituals; this is my way of life." Youfu and I started to imitate her, bending at the waist with palms together and followed her chanting even though we did not understand the meaning of the words. When I was a little older, I understood that one of the main principles in Buddhism is that all beings are afflicted with suffering, but you can aspire to end suffering for yourself and others by living according to kindness, generosity, and openness. She taught us to practice mindfulness at all times, not to be judgmental, and to live the "middle way," as a path of moderation between the extremes of sensual indulgence and self-mortification.

Grandma also told us that Buddhists believe in reincarnation, that people are reborn again after dying. They believe that people continually go through the cycle of birth, life, death and rebirth. She practiced compassion not only with her family and friends but also with our neighbors, and even total strangers. We were poor, but we always had shelter and food to eat. We did not have fish and meat often, maybe once a week with stir fry vegetables and shredded pork or steamed fish. But Grandma never touched any meat or fish. She ate only tofu, beans, rice and vegetables. Sometimes we would notice a beggar at the door; Grandma would always give a bowl of our food to anyone who appeared at our door.

The door to our home was always open except during the winter months when it was very cold. Neighbors would visit us by just announcing, "Is Youfeng's mother home?" or "Is

Grandma home?" as they walked right into the hallway and kitchen area. It was perfectly all right for neighbors to visit each other without previous arrangement and for children to play together in the courtyard and run into each other's houses during the day without their parents' permission. Our neighborhood functioned like a huge extended family.

But sometimes, behind closed doors, our parents and grandmother practiced traditional rituals in our home according to the Chinese lunar year calendar, especially on New Year's Eve in January or February. Following our grandma and parents' examples, we would line up in front of our family alter and kowtow three times one-by-one to our ancestors before our special meal. We believed in the existence of our ancestors' souls and worshiped them. We also believed our ancestors would watch over us and protect us from heaven. But we did not want our neighbors to know that we were practicing this ancestor worship ritual for fear that someone might report us to the neighborhood committee.

Usually very thrifty, my family went all out for the New Year's Eve dinner. We usually had "eight treasured items" (that included dates, peanuts, red beans, several kinds of preserved fruit, and sweet rice), "lion head" (meat balls), a whole duck, a whole chicken, a whole fish, mouth-watering steamed lotus root with sweet rice inside, sweet fruit soup for dessert and three to five stir-fried vegetable side dishes.

During the rest of the year, we often went without many things just to save for this annual feast. No matter how hungry and how badly we children wanted to eat, our parents would always invite our ancestors to eat first. Mother would murmur prayers while we all waited patiently. This was a time of great anticipation as the fruity sweet smells of the cooked delicacies on the table floated through the house and under our noses.

When we finally sat down to eat, Mother would say, "Eat as much as you can, but save the fish head and tail." We all knew what that meant. The Chinese phrase "You tou you wei" (to have both a head and tail), means you will have a good beginning and a good end; the fish, "yu", also means "abundance". We stuffed ourselves with our favorite dishes, but saved the fish head and tail for the next day's soup. We ritually saved them to symbolize "a good beginning and a good end" for the coming year and in the hope for abundance and a good harvest. The leftovers from this annual New Year's Eve feast lasted the whole family for two weeks. This was the traditional feast our family practiced for generations.

Grandma taught us to be honest and to show compassion for all creatures, even the smallest ones. Sometimes Youfu and I played together and watched ants moving food from one place to another. We would spend hours watching and wondering how all these little creatures lived and survived. Grandma would warn us, "Just watch them. Do not touch them. Do not kill them. They have lives, too."

When admonishing us, Grandma would say, "There is always a wise being watching you three feet above your head. Whatever you do, it will be recorded." So my elder brother and I always tried to behave and do our best. Of course, being a boy, my elder brother sometimes forgot.

One afternoon, Youfu and I were helping to get the table ready for dinner. I wiped the table while Youfu placed five pairs of chopsticks on the table and poured some rice wine into a small cup for our father. Without warning, he quickly sipped a little rice wine from the cup and smacked his lips when there were no adults around. I warned him that Dad would notice that the cup was not as full. "Bu-but-uh-I-i-ca-can a-a-add a-ah-l-li-ttle w-w-water in-into th-the c-cu-cup" he stammered. Luckily, Dad didn't notice any change, or he didn't say anything even if he had noticed. I just kept quiet.

My younger sister, Oufeng (Lotus Phoenix) was born in May 1955. It was the time of year when lotuses bloomed everywhere in Shanghai. My parents and Grandma always discussed children's names together as soon as a child was born. They named her for the beautiful white and pink lotus flowers. In Buddhist symbolism the lotus is symbolic of purity of body, speech and mind. Rooted in mud, its flowers blossom on long stalks as if floating above the muddy waters of attachment and desire.

Oufeng was a big baby and weighed nine Jin (about 11 pounds) when she was born. She slept a lot and grew fast. My mother had a lot of breast milk for Oufeng. Our neighbor in house No. 9 had a new-born son who cried day and night. We could hear him crying loudly from our house (No. 7) late at night when we had our windows open.

One day, our neighbor brought her son to see our grandma. She said, with tears in her eyes, "Grandma, I don't know what's wrong with my son. He doesn't sleep enough and cries all the time." My grandma put the baby on our kitchen table gently. With her magic hands, she felt the child's forehead and pulse. After checking the baby, she said simply, "There is nothing wrong with the baby. He is just hungry and that's why he cries all the time."

The boy's mother was very thin and had not fully recovered from childbirth. Therefore, her body could not produce enough milk to feed the baby. The baby did not like to drink cow's milk, so my mother offered to give some of her milk to the neighbor's boy and that stopped the crying.

Like Grandma, my mother was also respected in our little community. Since my father was making good wages as a dye-master, my mother could stay home to take care of her children. She often took in other children whose parents were both working long hours. She never accepted money from these families. In return for her kindness, these families would always bring our mother fresh fish, chicken and eggs for our table. These were considered much sought-after luxuries at that time.

After Grandma returned to her home in fall of 1955, I became the primary babysitter for Oufeng. One winter afternoon, I was holding her in my arms while walking her slowly in the warm sunshine in front of our house. Suddenly, Oufeng lurched out of my arms over my right shoulder and fell to the ground. I was terrified that she had been hurt and I started to cry. However, she turned out to be fine. She was wearing a thick padded jacket and pants as well as a woolen hat. She was so bundled up for the cold in these clothes that they cushioned her fall and she just bounced when she hit the ground.

The neighbor across the courtyard saw us and rushed over to help me pick Oufeng up. Oufeng cried briefly and stopped, but I was still sobbing. Our neighbor, Big Aunt (all children in our neighborhood called her Big Aunt) spent most of her time calming me down and assuring me that my sister was all right. She patted my sister and dusted off her clothes, and brought us into the house to tell my mother.

Mother was busy preparing dinner. After inspecting Oufeng carefully, she said to me, "Your sister is getting bigger and heavier each day. You should not hold her like that anymore." I promised my mother that I would be more careful, and I did not receive the usual punishment of going to bed without dinner.

Punishments for bad behavior included going to bed without dinner, receiving 10 to 30 strokes with a three-foot long, one-inch thick bamboo rod, and writing a "promise" not to repeat the behavior. The punishment depended on the seriousness of the infraction. I was sent to bed without dinner only once, when I dropped and broke two rice bowls while washing them.

My dad loved us very much, but he disciplined us strictly every time we stepped out of line or got into trouble. He kept his bamboo stick behind the door. Every time we did something wrong, he would point to the bamboo stick and we had to fetch it for him. If we sincerely promised not to transgress again and meant it, he would let us go the first time. But the second time there was no excuse and we would receive a bamboo beating on our bottoms.

Youfu got more than his share of punishment because he was the oldest and the naughtiest one in our family. At one time or another, he managed to receive every kind of punishment we had. Once, when he was about 10, he received a 30-bamboo-stick beating on his bottom for stealing some grocery money from Mama's pocket and buying candy on the way to school.

Actually, I was the one who told Mama that he had stolen the money because he had told me where the money came from while he was sharing his candy with me. I had no idea that he would receive such a severe punishment from our father or I would not have reported it.

Youfu could not sit down for several days after this beating. This punishment was the most severe ever handed out by our father, but it made an honest man out of Youfu. He never stole anything again after that incident. This also affected me and the other children greatly. I made up my mind on the spot never to lie or steal. I think my father meant for the rest of us to learn from Youfu's unfortunate example. There is an old saying, "Sha Ji Jing Hou" (killing the chicken to frighten the monkeys) meaning to punish someone as a warning to others. My father followed this old saying meticulously.

The Sunday after I dropped Oufeng, my father built a little three-wheeled wooden cart for my younger sister so that I could push her around instead of holding her in my arms. It worked perfectly, and we used it for two more babies. My dad was a skilled handyman and an excellent craftsman. He could build or repair anything. He also built two more beds in the attic as new children were added to our family.

Dad was a self-made man. His name was Baohua (Treasure of China). My father's father had died young and widowed our paternal Grandmother Shen in her early 30s. She had only one son and one daughter. Her daughter, Bao Zhu (Treasured Pearl) was two years younger than my father and was carried away in a big flood with many others in Shaoxing when she was only 12 years old.

Many years later, when I asked my father how this could happen to his sister, he said, tears welling up in his eyes, "It was in spring and we used to have heavy rain for a few days. But that spring my father had just died and it rained forever as if the sky was falling. Your grandma and I were trying to save our vegetables in the fields and left my younger sister home alone doing her needlework. Suddenly, we heard the roaring of the river water rushing through the fields and we ran as fast as we could towards our home. But when we got there, our house was gone; so was my sister. She must have been carried away by the flood."

My father, aged 14 then, searched for his sister all over the countryside and by the rivers and canals near Shaoxing for over a year, but he never found her. One year later, in summer of 1924, when he was 15 years old, my father finally gave up searching and left his hometown to apprentice himself to a textile factory in Shanghai. He travelled 120 miles to Shanghai to begin his career.

My father experienced some harsh treatment for the first few months as an apprentice. But he was tough and worked extremely hard to earn respect from the boss and other workers. After three years, at age 18, he became a master worker. Twenty years later, he developed specialized technical skills in dying traditional fabrics and was promoted to be a foreman in the same factory where he had started as an apprentice. Everyone called him "Ta bizi Shen Shifu" (Flat Nose Master Worker Shen), a typical nickname, as he had a flat bridge on his nose. By then, he was making more than 80 yuan a month, about double a regular worker's wage.

When my father learned his mother was sick, he asked for two weeks' leave and went back to his hometown to take care of her. When my grandmother was better, my father persuaded her to come to Shanghai. At first, she said she didn't want to live in the city, but when my father told her that my mother was expecting their first baby, she was very pleased. She said she could be useful to the family.

I vaguely remember her when she must have been in her early 60s. She had grey hair and very small feet. She slept a lot and I often played by her bedside. When I was about six, she became very ill and died in her sleep. I didn't know what illness she had; I just remember my elder brother and I cried a lot after she died and my parents were very sad.

On the day we went to the countryside to bury my father's mother, my mother braided my pigtails in a hurry. One of the pigtails felt too tight. She was busy getting everyone ready, so I redid my pigtail myself and tied it with the white yarn. (In China, the color white is the symbol of mourning.) Mother said, "It's a little twisted. Do you want me to help you?" I said, "No, Mama. I am fine." Then I ran out to join my elder brother to have my very first picture taken by a relative on this sad occasion. I remember this vividly even to this day. Whenever I look at these old photos, all the memories rush to my mind as if they had their own life, breaking through the flood gate, and I just can't stop them.

Both my parents were sad for a long time. My dad had lost the last member of his family of origin, but he had us now, so he was content with his life.

Whenever Dad came home from work, I used to find his slippers and then climb up onto his lap. Sometimes he would sing Shaoxing opera while holding one or two children on his lap. My mother always had our dinner and a two-ounce cup of warm rice wine with a small side dish of dried fish, soy beans or peanuts ready for our father when he came home from work. Dad never liked to drink his wine alone and always wanted us to join him. He often held one of us on his lap and let us lick drops of sweet rice wine from his chopsticks. He often gave us some soy beans or peanuts to chew from his small dish. Thirty-five years later, after we all grew up, he performed this same ritual with all of his grandchildren.

I believe we filled the void left in his heart by his own father's early death and his sister's disappearance and his mother's recent death. Sometimes when we quarreled or fought, Dad would say, "You children should be happy with what you have. Look at me. I don't have any sisters or brothers. You need to cherish each other and be good to each other."

One night after he said this, I had a dream. I dreamed I was fighting over something with my younger sister and hit her head with my fist and accidently killed her. I cried so much in my dream that I woke myself up. I was greatly relieved to find my sister lying sound asleep beside me. I have always treated her well ever since.

My parents and my grandmothers were very special people. They taught us how to be decent human beings. I am most fortunate to have grown up in the bosom of such a secure and stable family. I am amazed when I realize that my childhood stability existed in the midst of extremely turbulent times in China.

I was taught to be truthful, gentle and kind to my family and everyone in our community, even to strangers, little animals and insects. I was too young to realize the importance of this training, but I know now that this kind of love we felt and the responsibility practiced towards one another was the glue that bound us together so closely over the years. It also protected us from disasters many times over during the tumultuous events that were to unfold around us in the years to come.

Youfeng Shen

2 – The Flowers of New China
1956-1960

Despite the political upheavals and movements that occurred in China during my childhood and adolescence, our schools still managed to provide a solid formal education from elementary school to the third year of middle school in the cities of China. Education has always been highly valued among the Chinese people. Teachers, often called "the engineers of the human souls," were venerated and very much respected. Nevertheless, educational opportunities for working-class people, particularly for girls, were limited and illiteracy among the common people was high before the Revolution. This changed after the establishment of the People's Republic of China. The pupils of my generation, those entering elementary school in the 1950s, were seen as the hope and future of the New China and were referred to as "the flowers of New China."

On September 1, 1956, two months before my eighth birthday, I entered Xuhui District No. 2 Central Elementary School of Shanghai. As a city girl, I attended the neighborhood elementary school which was about a 10-minute walk from my home.

My school was one of the best elementary schools in the Xuhui district. It had two large classroom buildings, two playgrounds, one meeting hall, and a small canteen which served mainly the teaching staff. It accommodated about 1200 pupils, taught by 35 to 40 teaching staff.

Across the street from our school was Xujiahui Catholic Cathedral. Built of red bricks in 1906 in the Gothic style, this cathedral is still standing today and remains one of the largest places of religious worship in Shanghai. The cathedral was empty in the 1950s, as was the attached orphanage and school. Mother told me that when the Da Bizhi ("big-nosed foreigners") left in 1949 the orphans were sent to a government school run by the Communist Party. The new government had expelled foreign missionaries of all religious sects from China when the Communist Party took over in 1949.

Today the orphanage and school buildings are part of the Shanghai University campus and are used for evening and extension classes. The cathedral has been reinstated as a place of worship by the Catholic Church. It is also a well-known historical site visited by many foreign and Chinese tourists.

I remember the morning I started school. It was hot and humid—typical of the end of a Shanghai summer. People called this season the "Autumn Tiger" because it was ferociously hot like a tiger. The humidity hung so thick in the air that even the walls of our kitchen appeared to sweat.

After breakfast, Mother gave me a brand new school bag made from strips of different scraps of leftover fabrics with my name embroidered on the top center of the bag, a new white cotton blouse, and a cotton skirt with red and yellow roses on it. Mother smiled as she handed these to me.

"Today is your first day of school. Grandma and I made these for you for this special day. Now put on your new clothes, and I will take you to school."

I was so excited! I remembered Mother and Grandma had been sewing by hand before Grandma left Shanghai, but I had thought they were making new clothes for the baby. When I changed into my new blouse and skirt, I felt very special. I had never received three new items all at once in my whole life. It was like Chinese New Year again, when all the children in my family received two new items: a new top and a pair of new shoes.

Mother walked me to school that first day. Our neighbor Mrs. Zhu, who had agreed to watch my 15-month-old sister Oufeng and my almost four-year-old brother Yougen, brought them as far as the front gate of our lane where they waved goodbye to us. After a few blocks Mother and I passed an old shopkeeper selling his wares outdoors under a big fig tree. He knew my mother well and greeted her, "Good morning, Mama Shen. This must be your daughter. Look, how pretty she is! Just like a butterfly."

Mother replied proudly, "Yes, this is my oldest daughter. She is going to school today." The old man offered me some candy in a brown paper bag. I looked at Mother. Mother nodded and said, "Ok, you can have some candy today." Mother never spent money on sweets, so I took only one candy from the bag and left the rest. Mother encouraged me, "Take another one. Your younger sister cannot eat candy yet." So I took another one and happily followed Mother to school while sucking the precious sweet juice from the candy. I felt like I was indeed a butterfly. I jumped and danced all the way to school while holding my mother's hand.

Mother found my classroom and took me to meet my teacher. Mrs. Zheng saw us and came to greet us and shake our hands. She then showed me my seat. Mother said, "I have to go and get the children. Be a good girl and listen to your teachers." I nodded and waved goodbye to her. As she hurried out of the classroom, I could see tears in her eyes. Mother had never had the chance to go to school when she was my age.

Although Mother had been through an adult literacy program in the early 1950s and could write hundreds of characters and popular Chinese family names, she still couldn't read the newspapers or magazines. You need to know at least 2,000 to 3,000 characters to be able to read the newspapers and magazines. There are over 50,000 Chinese characters, though a comprehensive modern Chinese dictionary lists about 20,000 characters in use. An educated Chinese person will know about 8,000 to 10,000 characters. Regarding the difficulty of memorizing over 2,000 characters, there is no alphabet native to Chinese. But the characters have their own logic, which helps memorizing the rules and meanings of strokes made.

I was so happy to be able to go to school just like my elder brother. Mrs. Zheng was my primary teacher and taught us Chinese. She was in her early 30s and was a very caring and gifted teacher. With delicate features, a pair of gold-rimmed glasses, and an elegant grey silk dress, Mrs. Zheng stood out from other female teachers, who were all dressed in drab-colored cotton blouses and trousers.

Our math teacher, Mr. Liu, was a middle-aged man with a beard. He had a strong Suzhou accent and could not pronounce

Putonghua (common speech) very well. Fortunately, Mr. Liu taught us math, so it was not critical that he pronounce Putonghua accurately. I was soon to discover he was a very strict, but patient, teacher. He taught math for the whole first grade, which was composed of five classes of 35 to 40 students each.

We received two textbooks, a Chinese language book and a math book, as well as two notebooks for our math and Chinese homework. The moment I touched and smelled the crisp new textbooks and notebooks, I was thrilled as I had never received so many new books before. As soon as I got home, I carefully made book covers for the textbooks with a piece of white paper and wrote my name on the front of each cover.

During our first Chinese class, Mrs. Zheng taught us Pinyin, which is the Romanization of the Chinese characters based on their pronunciation. Pinyin literally means "spell sound" and was introduced in elementary school in the 1950s in order to improve literacy rates as well as to standardize the pronunciation of Chinese characters. We learned four initials, "b, p, m, f," in our first class and listened, repeated and practiced the Pinyin over and over again with Mrs. Zheng. During our second class, we learned how to write in our brand-new notebooks the four Pinyin we had just learned. After that, we practiced writing our own names. Mrs. Zheng checked our writing postures, the way we held our pencils, etc. She checked our writing one by one and showed us how to erase our mistakes without making a mess.

After second class, we went out to the playground to do the morning exercise called "Radio Calisthenics for Primary School." All students, teachers and even the Principal were lining up and following the rhythm of the music and moving arms, shoulders, heads and legs. There were two P.E. teachers on the platform demonstrating the movements for the new students, so we watched and followed their movements. I had an overwhelming feeling for the first time in my life to be one of over a thousand people doing exercises together while following the rhythm of the music and movement. I felt like I was a drop in an ocean of people doing something fun and magical. It made me feel really good to be part of something so great and spectacular, especially the last movement when all of us jumped and clapped our hands above our heads in unison.

After the morning exercises, we returned to our classroom and had our math class. Mr. Liu taught us how to write numeral numbers and do some simple counting. In the afternoon, we had music and P.E. classes. I never thought school could be so exciting and fun. My first day of school was really special.

Every morning, I couldn't wait for the school to open its doors. I loved all the classes and activities in our school. Mrs. Zheng always encouraged us and smiled a lot, even when we made mistakes. Her eyes sparkled behind her gold-rimmed glasses whenever one of us answered questions correctly. She treated all her pupils as if they were her own children. We often felt she was a second mother to us. Even years after I graduated, I would go back to school to see her as often as I could. She was the first teacher who inspired me to become a teacher. From the time I entered the first grade, I wanted to be a teacher just like her.

We also had some excellent music and art teachers in our school. Miss Chen taught us music and dance. Although we only attended her classes twice a week, I wished we could have had more lessons with her. Before each class, we lined up at the entrance of the music room and marched towards our seats one-by-one while she played our favorite music on the piano. She taught us folk songs and dances, and we gave performances for the whole school at the end of each term.

Our principal, Mrs. Wang, was our neighbor. She and her husband and their four children lived on our lane. Her husband worked at a publishing house in downtown Shanghai translating French books into Chinese and vice-versa. Because of their respected positions, they had a whole house to themselves. Their children went to the same school with us and one of their sons became my younger brother's classmate and best friend.

My favorite pastime after school was to play teacher with my younger siblings as pupils. I would set up a makeshift classroom at home and teach them what I had learned in school that day. I combined baby-sitting with mimicking my teachers. Sometimes, even the neighbor's children would join my little classroom. When my older brother Youfu had finished his chores, he also joined my little class and played his bamboo flute for us. We clapped our hands and sang with the music.

Youfu had learned to play the flute from one of his classmates, and later, he taught me how to play it, too. Back then, bamboo flutes were pretty cheap. They were the only musical instrument my family could afford. Youfu and I played together while the other children sang. We always had a good time with each other as well as with our neighbors' children.

I imitated my teacher Mrs. Zheng as closely as I could — her way of speaking, her mannerisms, and the way she conducted her classes. Fascinated by her knowledge and wisdom, I wanted to be just like her when I grew up. I taught my siblings and neighbors' children everything I learned at school, including songs and dances, and we sometimes gave performances in front of our home while our neighbors watched.

First and second grade pupils usually spent one or two hours per day after school doing homework assignments. The higher the grade, the more time you spent doing homework after school. I was usually focused when I did my writing assignments. I had to remember the order of every stroke in each character and write the same character 12 times. If you made one mistake, even a tiny dot in the wrong place or an extra line, you had to erase the whole character with an eraser and rewrite it carefully without leaving any trace of the mistake. Some pupils would make a mess if they didn't wash their hands before doing their homework or used an old eraser or a darker pencil. Then they had to repeat that character many times to get it right.

If I was completely focused on my homework and didn't have any interruptions, I could finish my Chinese assignments in about one hour and a half, writing Chinese characters and making sentences using new vocabularies and so forth. Then I would spend about half an hour doing the math assignments. But if I was not focused or was interrupted in any way, it was very difficult not to make any mistakes. If we made even a small mistake, we had to write that character 24 times the next day, or sometimes fill a whole page (108 times). It would take at least one hour just to correct those mistakes and another one or two hours to do new assignments. If a student didn't learn to get it right the first time, homework would continue to "snowball" and some children could never catch up. They had to repeat the same grade if they never caught up.

We used a lot of memorization in the first and second grades. This was the way Chinese children had learned to write their first few thousand characters for generations, and they are still doing it today. Most children had to be very focused and disciplined to be able to survive in the Chinese educational system. If someone had ADD or ADHD or any other learning disability, it was their problem and their parents' problem. There was no special program for those children. They either passed or failed and had to repeat the same grade.

There were often school-wide contests in poetry, song composition, and art. I remember winning first place in a poetry writing contest when I was in second grade. I won a notebook, two pencils and a toy wooden duck with wheels that made a funny "quack, quack" sound when I pulled it. This wooden duck was the only toy I ever owned during my entire childhood, and I really cherished it. I proudly pulled it "quack, quack, quacking" around the neighborhood after me for a couple of years.

I hadn't really felt deprived without toys though, because hardly anyone had toys. In my family of six children, we only had two toys in our house during our childhood. One was my wooden duck and the other was a small bamboo rattle. We shared these two toys with each other and as we each outgrew them, they were passed on to the younger children until they were broken into pieces.

As we progressed in school, we learned to perform more difficult tasks that carried more responsibilities. Since I performed well in school and received good marks in Chinese and math, I was nominated as the class monitor in second grade. The class monitor was responsible for assisting the teacher by collecting homework, calling "stand up" when any teacher entered the classroom, and reporting to the grade monitor when there was a school-wide rally. Grade monitors were responsible for the whole grade. Each class had 35 to 40 pupils, and there were four to five classes in each grade.

At the end of each term a rally was held for the entire school. Each class monitor would report to the grade monitor and each grade monitor would then report to the principal.

I still remember what I said to the grade monitor over 50 years ago as I saluted him: "I, Youfeng Shen, monitor of Class One, Grade Two, hereby report to the grade monitor, Xiaowen Wu. In our class of 38 pupils, 37 are present, only one absent. That's all." Wu wrote down the number in his notebook, saluted me back and said, "Your report is received. Thank you."

All of the class and grade monitors were "Hong Ling Jin" ("Young Pioneers") and wore red scarves. About half of the pupils in my class belonged to the Young Pioneers; we got a red scarf to wear once we were accepted. Those of us who belonged to the Young Pioneers proudly wore our scarves around our necks and saluted one another when performing duties. Pupils were not eligible for the Young Pioneers until they were in second grade and had shown they were good students with good behavior and good grades.

During my second grade, I was also given the responsibility of writing the weekly school news bulletins—announcements and stories for the whole school. These items were written on two big blackboards at the entrance to our school. One was for the fourth through sixth grades and the other for the three lower grades, which I was in charge of.

I was chosen because Mrs. Zheng considered my Chinese character writing to be neat and well-formed. Each week the class monitors in the lower grades collected written information from their classes and passed it on to me to edit and transfer to the big blackboard. I had to find other students to help me draw pictures and write the Chinese characters on the board because it was a very time-consuming job and too much work for one child.

Alone, it might have taken me three or four hours to complete this task, but with helpers it only took about two hours. I could usually find helpers because we had fun working together trying to arrange the layout on the board for the eight to ten items we usually received. We used different colored chalk and drew pictures to illustrate or emphasize the various pieces. Mrs. Zheng also helped with editing and checked our work. Sometimes it was hard to find helpers, especially before mid-term and final examinations, but I only ended up doing this task alone once over a two-year period.

It was the end of summer vacation, just before fall term began. I received some announcements and a few messages from our teacher to put on the blackboard. I couldn't find anyone to help me because it was summer vacation. My elder brother Youfu agreed to help me draw pictures, but it still took me nearly three hours to finish all the writing. Youfu had finished his drawings in about an hour and left. I was still working on my last piece two hours later when Mrs. Zheng came to check on me. She noticed that I was sweating and my face was flushed. She felt my forehead and asked me to stop and take a break. But

I was determined to finish everything before taking a break. She said gently, "Youfeng, I believe you are running a fever and you need to stop now. I am going to take you to the clinic."

"But I have just a few more lines. I will be done in a few minutes," I replied stubbornly and continued writing. I did not notice that I was feeling bad until I had finished the last character. My arms and legs were sore and I had a headache.

Mrs. Zheng immediately took me to the local clinic, got me some medicine and then took me home. My mother had just given birth to my youngest sister Xiao Mei the month before and was still recuperating as my grandma had to leave early for another birth this time. Mother was grateful to Mrs. Zheng for taking care of me and tried to give her money for the medicine and doctor's fees. But Mrs. Zheng refused and said, "Youfeng got sick because she worked too hard for the school assignment. I should have stopped her sooner but she was too stubborn. Please let me pay for this." Then she gave my mother my medicine and left.

I remembered this kindness later on when I was a teacher and tried to treat my own students with as much caring and consideration as Mrs. Zheng had shown me. Looking back, I now realize that it was excellent basic training that prepared me well to build language and organizational skills for my future work as a student and teacher.

My third and fourth grade teacher was Mr. Dai. He was in his early 40s, but looked much older because he had a beard and a mustache. Mr. Dai was also a very kind and remarkable teacher. He visited each student's home during his first few months with us, talked to our parents and got to know all his students' families. This was not required, but typical for dedicated elementary school teachers. My parents respected him a great deal. He gave us challenging assignments and homework. I enjoyed his teaching styles and his challenging assignments. But I still found time to read ahead in the fifth-grade books, which my elder brother brought home.

We did not have a lot of books at home, but Youfu and I often went to the public library to borrow; we were allowed five books each, every time we went. Every night, I sucked up the magic of these books like a sponge, I hated it when my mother turned off the light and made us go to sleep. Sometimes I would get out a flashlight and continue reading under the covers until she discovered me.

During one particular summer vacation, I was reading a novel about some young people working at a steel plant in Northern China. I was so involved with the main characters of the book that I wanted to go join them. I thought my life was very boring compared to their exciting lives. I wanted to leave home for an adventure, so I packed a bag of clothes, sneaked out of the house and headed toward the train station. But when I got there, I realized I had neither an address to go to nor the money to purchase a ticket. Even with the book in my hand, I didn't know how to ask the adults the way to that steel plant. When it got dark, I got scared and hungry. In the end, I came back home, very disappointed, and quietly unpacked my clothes. It's hard to believe now, but at the time I couldn't tell the difference between the fictional characters in the book and reality; I thought they were real people. I told no one about this incident until 30 years later. When I finally shared this experience with my little sister, she told me she had a similar experience when she was about the same age.

My fifth and sixth grade teacher was Mr. Huang, who was in his late 20s. He was tall and handsome. Like most of the other girls in our class, I developed a crush on him. When we found out he had a girl-friend who was still studying at a teachers' college, we were all disappointed. Mr. Huang had just graduated from a teachers' college and our class was his first teaching assignment. He was a good teacher, but he didn't have much experience in dealing with students, especially naughty ones.

As I was the monitor of the class, I always shouted as soon as the teacher entered the classroom, "Every one, stand up!" All students stood up and said in unison, "Good Morning, Teacher Huang!" The teacher replied, "Good morning every one. Please sit down." We started our classes like this for every class. Since I had a loud voice, some of the students in my class jokingly called me "loudspeaker". I didn't mind this nickname because I did have a loud voice, and I also wanted all students to hear me and stand up at the same time to show our respect and promptness.

One morning, during Mr. Huang's class, my desk mate, Pingping, took my only pencil without telling me. We all shared a bench and desk with another student because our desks had two separate built-in tops that lifted up so we could store our school bags, books and pencils inside. When I needed to write something down, I couldn't find my pencil. I noticed Pingping was using my pencil, so I raised my hand and told Mr. Huang that Pingping had taken my pencil without telling me. Mr.

Huang asked him to return the pencil to me. Pingping did so, reluctantly, but said under his breath, "You watch out!"

During the next class, we had an individual-study period for doing our Chinese assignment. While I was focusing on writing new characters we had just learned, Pingping purposely hit my elbow very hard with the side of his hand. He said, "Your elbow has just passed the 38th parallel." (The 38th parallel was the dividing line between Soviet and American zones during the Korean War.)

There was no teacher around, so I said to him, "You don't have to hit me so hard. I would have moved if you had just told me that my elbow had passed the line." My elbow really hurt and I tried hard to hold back my tears.

Just then, Mr. Huang passed by our classroom windows and heard my voice. Mr. Huang said sarcastically, "The loudspeaker of our class is broadcasting."

This was so unfair under the circumstances that I retorted, "Fang Pi" (bullshit)! Everyone in the class turned around to stare at me in surprise because I had never talked like that to anyone, even my classmates. How dare I talk to a teacher like that! Mr. Huang's face turned red at my sudden impertinence, and he ordered Pingping and me both to stay behind during our lunch break.

While all pupils went home for lunch, we were in Mr. Huang's office. Mr. Huang said to me, "I expected you to help him, but you fought with him instead." I explained that I didn't fight with Pinping. It was Pingping who had taken my pencil and then he hit me. I showed Mr. Huang my elbow, which was still red. Pinping couldn't deny this and he mumbled, "Her elbow passed the 38th parallel..."

Just then, I heard my mother's voice in the hallway. The other kids must have told her that I was in the teacher's office. She entered the teacher's office and said to Mr. Huang, "My daughter had only one bowl of porridge for breakfast this morning. She must be hungry now. Why do you keep her in school? Did she do something wrong?"

Mr. Huang replied, "I was just asking them what was going on. I must apologize for keeping her..."

Mother stopped him and said, "I don't like my daughter sharing the same desk and bench with Pingping anymore. He has already caused some trouble in my family when my daughter tried to help him after school. She is a child herself. I am taking my daughter home for lunch."

Ever since Mr. Huang assigned me to sit with Pingping and asked me to help him a few months before, I tried my best to help him by coaching him with his homework after school. Instead of doing his homework, he had given candy to my two younger sisters as a bribe for them to call me "Xiao bibi" (little vagina in Shanghainese). My five-year-old sister, Oufeng, knew it was a bad word and she shook her head and refused the candy. But my three-year-old sister, Xiao Mei, didn't know any better, took the candy and called me, "Xiao Bibi." I was very angry at her, but I knew she wasn't to blame because she was too young to understand. My mother had overheard the incident, but she kept quiet. She wanted to know how I handled the situation. I just told Pingping to go home to finish his homework by himself. But Mother knew Pingping was a bad influence on my younger siblings, so she didn't want me to coach him after class anymore.

I had felt sorry for Pingping because he was not well-cared-for at home and was always dirty. But he was disruptive in classes and mean to other children as well. When I went back to school after lunch, Mr. Huang had changed our seats. Pingping was given a new seat in front of the class by himself so that Mr. Huang could observe him easily. I now shared a desk and bench with my friend, Aiming. She and I had shared a desk and bench through third and fourth grade. We had been good friends ever since first grade and naturally were very happy to sit together again.

At dinner time, I told my family what happened in school. My parents were surprised to hear that I said "Fang Pi" (bullshit) to my teacher. They wanted me to apologize to Mr. Huang for being rude. But Youfu supported me and said, "M-m-Mr. H-Hu-Huang de-des-deserved i-it. H-he sh-shouldn't m-ma-make f-fu-fun-of y-your l-lo-loud v-vo-voice. H-he sh-should kn-n-know w-wa-what's g-go-going on i-in c-cla-class." But my parents insisted that I either apologize to Mr. Huang the next day or write a note of apology after dinner. So, I wrote a note of apology and handed it to Mr. Huang the next morning.

From this experience, I learned at age 12 that I did not have to put up with anything I thought was not fair. I could stand up for myself when I was right and did not have to accept any unfairness or injustice from adults or authority. I also learned that I shouldn't be rude to teachers or anyone else. I needed to speak calmly and courteously even when I was angry. Ever since this experience, I have not been afraid of defending my rights, my family, or my friends in the face of unjust authority. It was a lesson that would come in handy in later years.

Youfeng Shen

3 – Hard Times
1958-1962

I was 10 years old in 1958 when Mao Zedong launched his ambitious campaign called "The Great Leap Forward." The purpose of the campaign was to transform China from an agrarian economy into a socialist society through rapid industrialization and collectivization.

Initially, it had little impact on my life. My world was my home, my school and our safe little neighborhood. However, by the time I reached the third grade, I was becoming more and more aware of what was going on around me and in my school and in the neighborhood.

At the beginning of the "Great Leap Forward," we were told that in a short time China was going to "catch up" with Russia, England and even the United States. While pursuing a policy of national self-sufficiency, the Communist Party set out to mobilize the whole country to work day and night by promising a better future.

Almost overnight, Peoples' Communes, consisting of many villages with thousands of families, sprang up across China. Children were placed in communal nurseries while their parents worked around the clock. People ate in the communal dining halls. In order to increase the industrial output, government ordered factories, communes and schools to make steel. People all over China collected old woks, pots and pans and anything metal they could find. They built small furnaces to melt them.

Everyone in our neighborhood wanted to help, as it was considered a patriotic act to build our country's resource base. I, too, joined my classmates and my family in scavenging for old scraps of metal, copper and iron and anything we thought would be useful to the cause of building a more powerful and modern country.

I remembered one nursery rhyme that we school girls sang as we skipped and danced over a long chain of rubber bands on the sidewalk:

"Dong ye zhao, Xi ye zhao,

Fei tong lan tie shi ge bao."

It means, "Searching east, searching west, scrap copper and rusted iron are our treasures."

My elder brother, Youfu, and I tried to look for any iron, steel and copper we could find to take to school. Someone had even removed the large iron entrance gate to our lane and contributed it to the cause. This gate had originally been installed by the people of the neighborhood during the Japanese occupation of Shanghai in the 1930s. At that time, it was locked each night to prevent marauding, drunken Japanese soldiers from entering our lane to rape our women and steal from us. After the war, it was no longer used and it always stood open. I don't think anyone missed it or even noticed when it was gone.

Youfu and I searched our entire neighborhood but found nothing. We ended up taking an old wok, some odd-sized spoons and a leaking copper hot water container from our home to school. Other children more or less did the same.

Our teachers taught us during the day and took turns working at the school furnace after hours to make steel. We called this kind of furnace built by unprofessional people a "backyard furnace."

During that period, my father worked two shifts at his factory, from six-thirty in the morning to ten-thirty at night. The first shift was his regular day job, and the second shift he worked as a volunteer at the metal-reducing furnace section of the factory to produce steel. Afterwards, he would return home completely exhausted, fall on his bed and go to sleep without even cleaning up or taking off his shoes. When this happened, I carefully removed his shoes and put a blanket over him so he could sleep until five-thirty the next morning. Sometimes, he came home from work smelling of some kind of chemical acid. I remember mother nagged him about this offensive smell.

This situation lasted for months in Shanghai and all across China. Everyone was fired up by patriotism in those days. We believed Communism would produce a utopia in China. There were loud speakers and broadcasting everywhere, in schools, factories, communes and military bases. Everywhere we went, we could hear the patriotic music, songs and newspaper editorials promoting new ideas, new policies and changes through loud speakers.

As soon as we entered our school, we would hear the song "Dong Fang Hong" (East Is Red), which everyone in China knew. Its translation is: "The East is red. The sun is rising. China has brought forth Mao Zedong. He has a plan to bring the Chinese people good fortune. Hooray! He is the people's great savior." We truly believed that Chairman Mao was our savior and if we worked hard enough together, we would achieve the ideal socialist utopian society, Communism, which would provide everything a person needed. We would be secure and free from want of any kind.

Since adults were working around the clock, we youngsters ate in a communal neighborhood dining hall that provided free meals for all. I remember sitting with my two brothers and two younger sisters around a big rectangular table. Across the table, another family of five children were sitting and waiting for food. Our mothers were busy helping in the kitchen and serving the food. We children were excited as it was like a huge extended family. There were about 12 tables in the room which was originally the Neighborhood Committee Conference Room. A few grandparents were also helping to serve the food. We had rice with stir-fry pork and green vegetables, plus a bowl of egg-flower soup, which was quite warm and delicious.

I often heard the phrase "beef and potatoes is communism". I wondered why "beef and potatoes" and why not "rice and pork chops"? These were, after all, the favorite food of my people, not potatoes and beef. I thought perhaps our allies, the Russians, liked to eat beef and potatoes and we were just copying them. We actually had a beef and potato dish with rice once at dinner time. We liked it, but not as much as pork chops. Sadly, this communal dining did not last long; when the food got scarce, our communal dining hall closed.

As early as 1959, things started to go wrong. In order to keep the furnaces going, people used every type of fuel from coal to wood. In some places, people even cut down the trees to feed the furnaces. Where iron ore was unavailable, they melted any steel objects they could get their hands on, including utensils, chairs, doors, bicycles and even farming equipment, all of which was to produce steel girders. However, most of the steel produced this way was impure and of poor quality and thus cracked easily. Even worse, tending to backyard furnaces in the communes denied the time and opportunity for peasants to produce food, starving many and directly contributing to the Great Famine that struck China only a year later.

I didn't understand any of this at first; I just remember I was always hungry when I was about 11. My whole family was hungry. We didn't have our regular bowl of rice with some meat or fish stir fry vegetable dish and a bowl of soup for dinner anymore. We changed our regular bowls into smaller ones and our mother had no oil to stir fry anything, let alone fish and meat which had disappeared from our kitchen table completely.

During the first famine year, I noticed my parents weren't wearing new clothes on New Year's Day like the rest of us. Their excuse was that they weren't growing, so they didn't need new clothes and shoes. But I could tell from their patched clothes and worn-out shoes, they needed them more than we did. But they would provide anything within their power for us while depriving themselves. That winter, we didn't have any dishes for our "feast" for the Chinese New Year. We only had a few vegetable dishes we saved and one dried and salted fish from the previous year's celebration. I didn't know until much later that we, as city dwellers in Shanghai, were not nearly as bad off as the peasants in the countryside who grew the food. I only began to realize the true extent of this disaster when I started to do research for this book.

The Great Chinese Famine was caused by a combination of adverse weather conditions, social pressure, economic mismanagement, and radical changes in agriculture imposed by government regulations. Many scholars have listed a variety of causal factors, including bad weather, reduction in sown acreage, and the government's high procurement. In some provinces, politically motivated decisions took precedence over common sense. No one dared to say anything against the government. Some communes faced the task of doing things which they were incapable of achieving, such as boasting unrealistic increases in grain output for fear of being criticized as not following the Party and Chairman Mao. Agriculture was neglected because priority was given to producing steel. Many peasants were exhausted from long hours looking for fuel, scrap iron, and iron ore to keep the furnaces going. When harvest time came, not enough people were working in the fields.

Researchers also suggested that overconsumption in the communal dining system was another cause of the famine. People would eat their fill at the beginning of a rationing period and then, when the food supplies ran out later on because there wasn't enough to last at that generous level for the whole period, people would go hungry or worse, starve to death.

The drastic decline in the national larder was magnified by two other unforeseen natural disasters that coincided with these management blunders. First, one of the worst floods of the century struck China in 1959, killing two million people and devastating the central agricultural regions along the Yangtze River. That same year, a major drought hit Northern China around Beijing and along the Yellow River.

Additionally, in 1959 the Soviet Union chose to withdraw financial and technical support and called in all their past loans from China. Instead of helping China and giving support during these hard times, the Soviet Union demanded that

China immediately repay everything she owed to the Russian government. Mao Zedong's solution was to procure much of the food that was harvested for export to raise the money to pay back this debt. Even though the Russian government may not have made this demand in order to add to the famine, their demand and Mao's response (to export food in order to raise money to pay Russia back) did impact the famine. After the government procured its quota for export and for distribution to the cities, the amount of food remaining in the countryside was often insufficient to feed the very people who had raised it, and, in a cruel twist of fate, they were the ones who suffered and perished the most.

These multiple disasters combined over the next three years to produce a devastating famine across China resulting in about 30 million deaths. Although I didn't know the magnitude of the tragedy at the time, I heard from adults that even Chairman Mao wept when he learned how many people were dying from starvation.

Even though urban dwellers did not suffer as much as the peasants in the countryside, we did suffer. I remember my young, growing body hungering day after day for food that was so scarce. Often times, sharp pangs of hunger tormented me day and night. I was only 11 then, but I felt like I was an old woman. I did not have the energy I used to have, and I lost interest in many things I had liked to do before. I did not sing and jump rope anymore.

My youngest brother Youfa (Prosperous) was born on September 28, 1959, in the middle of this famine. Youfa's name choice reflected everyone's desires in our family while the whole country was starving!

I remember that difficult summer before Youfa was born. We couldn't get any food from regular markets, and we couldn't afford food sold on the black market. Mother got sick from malnutrition while she was carrying Youfa. Because she didn't have proper food, she was pale and swollen. She struggled to feed her whole family while neglecting herself, which resulted in several severe attacks of vertigo, fainting spells, and vomiting preceded by ringing in her ears. My father would usually save a steamed bun from his lunch at work and force it into Mother's hand when he came home.

"Please eat it for the baby's sake, if not for your own," Dad would beg her. Mother would split it among us children, and she would keep just a bite. If Dad was not around, she wouldn't even keep that bite.

During that summer of 1959, when there was no school, we three older children wanted to help our parents. Youfu was 13 then, I was 11, and Yougen was only 7. We were told that Dad's factory had been raising pigs as their supplement to the workers' lunch supplies at the factory canteen. The factory would pay three cents for each jin (1.1 pound) of wild pig weed we could deliver. Usually there was wild pig weed everywhere in the suburbs of Shanghai, which were about one hour away from our home on foot. But that year we couldn't find any close by because people were so hungry they were eating the pig weed with their rice. We had to walk three hours to find patches of pig weed in the fields outside the city.

The three of us started early in the morning. We got up at five and packed our lunch: a piece of pancake (about three ounces of flour with some salt, made the day before) and some water. We left our house at about five-thirty. It was still cool early in the morning and people were sleeping. At about eight-thirty, we reached the fields where we found thick patches of pig weed here and there. Youfu showed us the best way to collect the pig weed. Following his example, we pulled out the pig weed root, shook the soil from the root, and then put the weed into our rice bags. The fields were still wet in the morning, so it was not hard to pull the weed out, but we had a difficult time shaking the wet soil from the roots.

Youfu was very fast; he could fill up his rice bag in a couple of hours. When his bag was full, we took a break, washed our hands in a nearby river and ate our lunch together. There wasn't much to eat as we had already taken a few bites out of our pancakes on the way to the fields. Our tummies were always empty and always making gurgling noises. Sometimes, we found some vegetable leaves and cucumber ends in the fields. We would wash them in the river and eat them with our pancake to fill our stomachs. We even tried to eat fresh pig weed, but it was hard to swallow without being cooked.

When there was more pig weed, Youfu took off his long pants, squeezed the weeds into his pants and tied the waist and the ends of both pant-legs with rubber bands. It became very hot by noon. Even with our straw hats on, we sweated so much that our shirts were soaking wet and stuck to our skin. The fields around us were like a huge hot oven; the ground was dry and hard in the hot sun. It became more and more difficult for us to pull the pig weed out without breaking off the roots. We wanted the roots because they weighed more. We usually stopped after four hours of working in the fields and started the journey back. It took us more than four hours to get home because we were tired and hungry, and we were carrying heavy loads. The extreme afternoon heat also slowed us down.

Our father's factory was about 15 minutes from our home, so we usually went there first to sell our weeds. There was an old man named Lao Liu (Old Liu), with a pair of thick glasses like the bottoms of Coca-Cola bottles, who would weigh our bags one-by-one using his handheld scales. Then he would carefully add them up with an old abacus. It usually came to 60 or 70 jin (about 65 to 75 pounds). Then, he would give us the money and waggle his fore-finger at us, "Now go home and give the money to your mother. Don't spend it or lose it on your way home."

"Yes, Uncle Liu."

We would run back home as fast as we could and report to Mother:

"Mama, we made one yuan, eight jiao and five fen today!" Or, "Mama, we made two yuan, one jiao and three fen today!"

With tears in her eyes, Mother would put the money away and say, "Thank Buddha, I am so blessed with such wonderful children. Just rest a little, and I'll get you some cold green bean soup!"

Then we would all clean up and wash our hands, and Mother would bring us each a bowl of cold green bean soup. There were only a few green beans floating in the soup, but it was the most delicious soup in the whole wide world to us.

One afternoon, it was extremely hot and humid. After we were done picking weeds, Youfu suggested we take a swim in the river to cool off. Immediately, both boys took off their shirts, jumped into the river, and began swimming happily under the hot sun. I had never been in the river before. I couldn't swim. But seeing them having a good time, I waded into the river, too. The moment my feet touched the river bed, I found out that I couldn't stand up. I tried to keep my balance, but the river current knocked me off my feet and I began to sink. I was scared and screamed, "Help! Gege, Help!" I cried while gulping down mouthfuls of dirty, brown river water. Youfu, a few yards away, heard me and swam towards me as fast as he could. He saw my pigtail first, which was floating on the surface of the water, reached out his arms and lifted me upright so that I could stand up on my feet. The water level was only up to my chest, and I would have been able to walk slowly in the water if I had known how to keep my balance. But by then I was so frightened that I just wanted to get out of the water as soon as possible. Youfu pulled me out of the river and went back to get our younger brother Yougen. They were disappointed because my unexpected accident had spoiled their fun.

Ever since that day, I have been scared of the water. I have never dared to go into any river again. But Youfu and Yougen continued to swim in that river for the rest of the summer. While they swam, I usually found a shady spot under the nearest tree and settled down to read. Unfortunately, that fall they both became very ill with liver flukes (fasciola parasites) from that dirty river water.

They suffered continual episodes of fever and chills and vomiting during their illnesses. One moment, they were so hot they were sweating, soaking their clothes and bedding. The next moment, they were so cold that their teeth chattered. They had to take very strong medications to recover. Fortunately, their medical bills were covered 80 percent by our father's medical benefits. But this illness caused permanent damage to Yougen's liver as he was only seven years old when he got sick. Because of that damage, Yougen couldn't pass the physical examination to become a pilot in the Air Force 15 years later. However, he was able to pass the less rigorous physical exam for the People's Liberation Army and joined the infantry later.

I was lucky that I stayed away from that dirty river; I did not get liver flukes. But I believe my health was a little damaged by those hungry years when I was growing up. I did not have my first period until I was 16 years old.

During that time, food was so scarce that even wealthy people suffered. The Communist government began a food rationing program in the cities at that time. We had rationing coupons for everything including cooking oil, tofu, eggs, fish, rice and meat. Each adult male laborer was allowed about 25 t0 30 jin of rice a month (about one pound per day). Adults who performed less intensive labor received coupons for 20 to 25 jin. Children received from 5 to 15 jin of rice monthly according to their ages. I remember I got about 12 jin of rice per month. In big cities like Shanghai and Beijing, the government honored the ration coupons, so people could get by. But in smaller cities and outlying rural provinces--such as Anhui, Sichuan and Jiangxi-- sometimes the local governments had no food or supplies and then were unable to honor the ration coupons they had distributed in their area of authority. Consequently, the coupons people worked so hard to save became worthless paper.

This coupon rationing system continued for more than two decades. Over the years, coupons were gradually retired for various items as they became more plentiful.

There were eight of us at home, and we lived our lives from one day to the next—adjusting, cooperating and doing our best to survive. A family of five or larger could receive one head of cabbage for the whole day's supply of vegetables. A smaller family with four or fewer members might receive only half a cabbage as their allotment. Trying to keep the family fed absorbed all of our energies each day.

I remember my mother cooking a big pot of rice with cabbage or whatever vegetables we could get at the market with our coupons. Then she often cooked another pot of tofu soup or egg soup as a side dish. For lunch or dinner we could only have one bowl of rice and a half-bowl of soup each. We had to save some of the rice for our breakfast porridge the next morning or go without breakfast. Sometimes we only had two meals a day consisting of a bowl of porridge at nine in the morning and a bowl of rice and a half bowl of soup at four in the afternoon.

On rare occasions, Mother was able to add a little salted pork or fish to the rice pot. The smell of salted pork or fish with rice and vegetables was so tempting that we sat around the kitchen table patiently waiting for dinner and savoring the odor of the cooking food. When dinner was served, we thought the food was the best food in the whole world. In order to get a few more bites of rice scraped from the bottom of the pot, my two brothers and I always fought for the job of cleaning the rice pot and the dishes after dinner. My parents made us take turns and never lacked volunteers for this kitchen chore.

I often dreamed to myself in those days, "If I could only have one more bowl of rice, I would be in heaven." When we were filling our one small bowl of rice for dinner, all of us kids packed the rice down as hard as we could to squeeze as much rice as possible into our bowls.

When we did this, our mother warned us, "Are you trying to break your bowl?" If we broke a bowl, we all knew it meant going without dinner as punishment and that our portion of rice would be saved to make the next day's breakfast porridge. So we squeezed our rice more carefully after that and never broke a bowl.

In the fall of 1959, our grandma was unable to come to Shanghai as usual to help with the birth of Youfa, because my grandfather was ill. She had to stay home to take care of him. For the first time my mother had to go to the hospital to deliver her baby. I later learned she also had her tubes tied at the hospital because she did not want any more babies.

Mother was 39 years old when she had that procedure. Family planning was being encouraged at that time by the Chinese government to reduce the overpopulation problem. Chairman Mao had made a major mistake in encouraging people to have more children. His slogan had been "the more the better". But now many people were starving as a result of this policy and the recent famine in China. I also think Mother was tired after 10 pregnancies and four miscarriages or childhood deaths. That was enough for anyone.

While she was in the hospital, somebody had to dump the night soil and clean out the ma tong (the family chamber pot). Nobody asked me to do this, but I knew it was my duty to assume my mother's chore as her eldest daughter. It was not considered "men's work"; women were expected to do it. It had always been my mother's first chore every morning, but now I was old enough and physically able to replace her, so I assigned myself this stinky, unpleasant task.

The distance from our house to the local sewage dump station was about a 10-minute walk down a narrow, cobbled street, which always seemed to have brownish puddles of rain water here and there. The ma tong was made of solid wood. It wasn't heavy when empty, but with night soil from the whole family in the pot, it weighed at least 30 pounds. I had to watch the road carefully to avoid the puddles in the street and also had to stop several times to rest along the way. As a result, the round trip took me about 30 to 35 minutes depending on the weather and how heavy the pot was.

When I approached the dump station the putrid smell emanating from the place made me sick to my stomach. The odor was strong enough to make anyone within 100 feet of the place retch.

The dump station consisted of a large, underground septic tank with an open hole in the top at ground level into which the night's sewage was dumped from hundreds of wooden ma tongs like ours. I knew that I had to do it in spite of the awful odor. When I was only a few yards away from the station, I held my breath, walked as fast as I could to the station, opened the pot lid and dumped the night soil into the tank. Then I grabbed the lid and rushed away as fast as I could, before I had to breathe again. I was always happy to be on my way back home from that smelly place. It was an easy job to clean the pot compared with the awful smell of the dump station. I just poured some water into the pot and used a bamboo brush to clean the inside. Then, I used a wet rag to clean the outside of the pot and left it and the rag to dry out in our backyard.

Even though I hated this job, I continued to perform it after my mother returned from the hospital. It was particularly onerous during the cold winter months when my hands were freezing and covered with chilblains so that my fingers looked like carrots by the time the pot was washed clean. I had no gloves or mittens to cover my hands, but I knew I had to do this for my mother so she could stay in bed a little longer and nurse my new baby brother, Youfa.

One particular morning, on my way to the dump station, it was snowing very hard. This was unusually harsh weather for Shanghai, as if heaven wanted to punish the starving populace even more. With careful, small steps on the icy and slippery cobble-stone street, I tucked in my head to keep the snow from pelting my face and chin. I was barely able to draw a breath without inhaling a mouthful of snow, and every gasp of freezing air cut into my lungs like a sharp knife. After I emptied the pot, I started to hurry home to get warm. The cobbled street was so slippery that I fell down on my bottom. My right hand, which carried the pot, was cut by the pot handle and was bleeding. I could not feel any pain from the cut. Fortunately, I did not break the pot or my hand, so I did not have to tell my mother about this incident. As soon as I cleaned the pot, I took care of my right hand and changed into a pair of clean pants. Mother was upstairs in the attic with the baby and I did not want her to have to worry about me.

When Youfa was about six months old, in the middle of the famine, my maternal grandfather came to visit us from Shaoxing; he had just recovered from his illness. He thanked our parents for sending them 10 yuan a month all those years. "Otherwise," he said to us, while slowly stroking his long beard, "your grandma and I would have died just like other poor village people." I sensed my mother was not happy to see him.

"Why did you come alone without Grandma?" my mother asked.

"She said she didn't want to bother you and she also wanted to save the train fare." Grandpa took off his long jacket and laid down on our dad's bed without taking his shoes off. Then he yawned and took a long nap while I helped Mother move Dad's stuff upstairs. We didn't know how long Grandpa would stay with us, but we children were prepared to sleep on the floor in the attic. Later I found out from Mother that he thought he could get some good food in Shanghai. But Mother told him he could only stay for a week because everything we bought from the stores was rationed and we didn't have anything extra.

Then Mother said coldly, "Every day you stay with us, you are taking food from your grandchildren's mouths."

Grandpa nodded his head and said, "Okay, I didn't know things were so bad here, too. I thought you would feed me since I just recovered from my illness."

"I will try my best, but look at all your grandchildren. Everyone is so thin. I can't even feed them." Mother started to sob, "Why didn't you write to us before coming?" There was no response from him, and I just left to do my homework in the attic.

The next day, Mother brought home a cookie with our last coupon of the month. We usually shared it with each other. But Grandpa saw it and said excitedly, "Wow, that's a nice cookie, is it for me?" With his long, dirty finger-nails, he grabbed it from our mother's hand and started to eat it at once while we children watched him chewing and enjoying his cookie as our mouths watered. Grandpa only stayed with us for one week, not two months as he wished. Thank God for this. Unlike Grandma, he expected to be waited on and served by our mother for all his needs. Mother never borrowed money or food from anyone, but this time she had to borrow some rice from our neighbor, Mrs. Zhu.

In the summer of 1962, when my youngest brother, Youfa, was almost three years old, my parents decided to try and find an adoptive home for Youfa. They had decided to do this to reduce the burden of the famine on our family. They also wanted to give him, the youngest and most vulnerable son, a better chance to survive the famine. In order to help us, one of my mother's friends introduced my parents to a wealthy childless couple who wished to adopt a male child. My mother and her friend took Youfa to a nice restaurant in the center of Shanghai business district to meet this couple.

Only very privileged or very rich people could afford a meal in a restaurant in those days. This couple treated my mother, her friend and Youfa to the most delicious dumplings and delicacies the restaurant could provide at that time. Everything went smoothly until it was time to leave and my mother forgot her handbag. She had been distracted by her emotions and had left it on an empty chair beside her. Youfa noticed it and piped up, "Mama, don't forget to take your handbag."

A few days later, the friend told my mother that this couple had liked my little brother very much but that they thought he was "too smart" to adopt. They thought that any three-year-old boy who could pay attention to his mother's handbag and try to take care of his mother in this way might very well be smart enough to run away and return home as soon as he grew a little older. They decided to find another, younger boy to adopt.

Years later, we were told that this family experienced great hardships during the turbulent times of the Cultural Revolution. Both parents were sent to different labor camps and their young adopted son was neglected and suffered a great deal. We were all glad that Youfa had stayed with us and was thus spared this persecution. But we felt sorry for the other boy who had taken Youfa's place.

Life wasn't all work and suffering, even in those difficult years. After the initial hunger pangs had passed, I got used to my shrinking stomach and eating less. To me it became a way of life. We just had to learn to live with it, and make the best of it.

I remember one cold winter night when we tried to sleep in our beds with empty stomachs. The attic bedroom was almost as cold as the freezing temperature outside because there was no fuel to heat our house. We wore as many layers of clothing to bed as we did during the day and cuddled close to each other. I always held my youngest sister's hands since her hands were colder than mine. Oufeng slept at the foot of the bed keeping our feet warm. Mother and our then three-year-old youngest brother

Youfa were sleeping in the other big bed. On this particular night, I remember that we heard a loud rumble from someone's stomach.

"Whose was that?" Oufeng asked.

"I don't know. But it is not mine," I responded.

"I think this is from my tummy," Xiao Mei answered. We all laughed and wondered how such a small person could produce so loud a sound.

One Sunday morning we had no school, so we all got up a little later than usual. After breakfast, Mother gave me some flour to make noodles for our dinner. I mixed it with some salt and water, kneaded the dough and flattened it out with a rolling pin. Then I cut it into long thin pieces and placed the long noodles on a piece of white paper to dry.

It was about six hours until dinner time and Xiao Mei was hungry. When no one was in the kitchen, she took two pieces of uncooked noodles from the table, hid under the kitchen table and ate them. When Mother came into the kitchen, Xiao Mei came out from under the table and said, "Mama, there were two bad people who came out of the sky and stole two noodles."

Noticing there was still bits of flour on Xiao Mei's lips, Mother said, "Where are the bad people from the sky now?"

"Oh, they just flew away," my sister said, pointing out the window.

"What happened to the noodles they took?" asked my mother.

"They're here," Xiao Mei replied seriously while pointing to her little mouth with her index finger. We all laughed at her because she was so funny, and everyone in my family still laughs whenever anyone mentions this incident from the hungry years.

When Xiao Mei was about five, tiny and very cute, our neighbor across the courtyard, Mrs. Zhu, decided she wanted to be her Godmother. Mrs. Zhu was a tiny woman herself, with a pock-marked face. She was a middle-aged woman whose son was already grown and had left home. Her husband worked in another city and only came home on annual vacations. Mrs. Zhu loved to come to our home and play with Xiao Mei and Youfa, freeing my Mother to get her chores done.

One day she asked my Mother, "Why are your two youngest ones so tiny and thin?"

Mother smiled sadly and replied, "No one is big and fat these days. After eight pregnancies, my body is worn out, so they were born smaller. There isn't enough food to feed them as much as I fed the older children. I couldn't produce enough milk for them either."

Mrs. Zhu said, "Why don't you let me take Xiao Mei home and feed her? I'd like to be her Godmother."

After that, Mrs. Zhu often took Xiao Mei to her house or brought a bowl of red bean soup, or anything she was cooking for her dinner in the late afternoon to our house to feed the two little ones. Sometimes I got home from school and smelled the delicious soup she was feeding them. I was so hungry that I craved a bit of food, even just a spoonful of soup. I wanted to ask for a little, but I held my tongue; I was almost 14 and thus old enough to control myself. Instead I would say "hi" and leave in a hurry before my stomach started making noises.

Even during the famine, once we got used to it, we were able to play. One game I enjoyed was table tennis. Ping pong has always been popular in China. We couldn't afford to buy a regular ping pong table, so we used our kitchen stools and borrowed the neighbor's stools to make a ping pong table. We used a bamboo stick in the center resting on top of two small bricks in place of the net. It was not easy to play ping pong on four (sometimes six) kitchen stools, but we lined up and eagerly awaited our turn to play. We had fun and we all got to be pretty good at playing ping pong on kitchen stools.

My childhood during these years was filled with trials, hardships, self-discovery, and the simple joys of life. All these left an indelible mark on my memory forever.

After the disastrous Great Leap Forward, Mao Zedong was forced to resign from his position as Head of State, but he remained in the position of Party Chairman. In 1962, Liu Shaoqi replaced Mao as Head of State and assumed the leadership of the government. Under Liu Shaoqi's leadership, our government immediately abandoned the Great Leap Forward and began to stabilize the economic situation in China.

Once the situation began to return to normal, some people protested, criticized and voiced their opinions openly about the failure of the government. But most people in our neighborhood, like my parents, never discussed or commented on the political situation. They were careful to avoid discussing or being involved in politics and never openly criticized the government. They just watched, kept their mouths shut and maintained a low profile. This was how most ordinary people survived repressive political infighting and upheaval in the government and protected their families.

My father always said, "It's better to be a Xiao Ren Wu (small potato) than a big shot. Just be happy with what you have. Tall trees catch the wind."

As a result of my parents' common sense, we all survived and eventually made it through the political changes in China. No one in our family was persecuted or sent away to a labor camp. We listened to our parents' advice and followed it closely because we trusted them. It never occurred to us to question their authority. Doing whatever our parents told us to do always worked for us.

No one survived the three-year-famine alone. It was the traditional cohesiveness of Chinese families and local communities that allowed the bulk of the Chinese people to survive during those lean years and the upheavals that followed.

These were the most difficult years in the history of China. Everyone suffered. Millions of people, especially people living in the countryside, died. We were lucky. We had each other and we survived.

Youfeng Shen

4 – Stepping Out
1962-1966

In 1962 a thorough reform of the school system, which had been planned earlier to coincide with the Great Leap Forward, went into effect. In connection with the Socialist Education Movement, the reform was intended as a work-study program in which schooling was slashed to accommodate the work schedule of communes and factories. It had the dual purpose of providing mass education at a low cost and of re-educating intellectuals to accept the need for their own participation in manual labor.

In accordance with this policy, some factories with the necessary resources in Shanghai had started their own "Gongye Zhongxue" (industrial middle schools). These schools were similar to vocational schools in the United States. I was almost 14 years old at the time and had just graduated from elementary school in June. I could go to a regular Middle School like my elder brother Youfu, or I could go to one of these new factory-run industrial schools. If I went to a regular middle school, my parents would have to pay six yuan a semester for my tuition. But if I went to a work-study program, I would receive three yuan a month from the factory. This would make a huge difference to my family.

With eight mouths to feed and our grandparents to support, my parents were still struggling and trying very hard to survive one day at a time. Considering the family financial difficulties at that time, my parents suggested that I go to one of the factory-run schools. As a good daughter and big sister to my siblings, of course I understood the situation and said "yes". But in reality I was sad. This meant I would never be able to go to a teachers' college, and my dream of becoming a teacher would never come true. I knew I should put our family needs before my own individual dreams, but I couldn't help feeling sad in my heart. To hide the tears running down my cheeks, I ran to the backyard to sit on the pot, pretending I was doing my business. I stayed there for over half an hour trying to bring my emotions under control.

From 1962 to 1965, I spent three years in the industrial work-study program run by Shanghai Number Eight Sweater Factory. The factory was located in downtown Shanghai. Every morning, I got up at six o'clock with my Dad. It took me about 45 to 50 minutes to walk to the factory. Of course, I could have taken a bus, which would only have taken about 10 minutes, but bus rides cost four fen (less than one U.S. penny). I did not mind walking. That way, I could give my mother the whole three yuan each month as soon as I received it from the factory. Once, mother gave me some change for my bus fare, but I didn't use it for the bus fare. Instead I saved it and went to see a movie for 10 cents with my classmate Weiwei who lived close to my home. But after that one time I always returned the change to my mother.

Weiwei and I always took Hengshan Road (the fastest way to our school) and walked to school and back home together. One day on our way home, we saw a five-fen coin on the ground. We fought over it, but Weiwei saw it first, and she took it. I thought it was fair since she had seen it before me. When we got close to her home, we said good-bye to each other as usual.

The next day, Weiwei didn't come to school. I wondered what had happened to her; maybe she was sick? I was planning to visit her after school, but we had to prepare for our math test for the first class next morning. I thought I would go and see her after the test for sure. Surprisingly, Weiwei showed up for the test next morning, wearing all white, which meant she was mourning someone's death. Her eyes were red and swollen from crying. I grabbed her hand and asked, "Weiwei, Wha–What happened?"

Weiwei sobbed, "My mother just died. She, she hanged herself. I shouldn't have picked up the money. I will never pick up money from the ground again."

I held her hand and said, "I am so sorry about your mother, but it had nothing to do with picking up the money. That's superstition." We often heard adults saying that it's bad luck to pick up stuff on the ground. Weiwei thought her mother had died because of her action.

Just then, our math teacher, Ms. Ding came over and said kindly to Weiwei, "You don't have to take the test today. I'll arrange another time for you to take the test. You still have two more days to stay home and recover from the shock."

But Weiwei said she wanted to take the test. She didn't want to be home alone. Her father was busy with all the funeral arrangements and her siblings were in the neighbors' care. Poor Weiwei at only 14 years old had to become the mother to her four siblings overnight. But she continued the middle school program and received good grades. She had great courage and was stronger than her mother who couldn't handle the difficult times and committed suicide, which devastated the whole family.

Weiwei carried on her mother's responsibilities and helped her father raise her two brothers and two sisters. I admired her very much for her bravery and strong personality. Weiwei and I became very close friends. I often stopped by her house after school to support her. Sometimes I would help with her chores when she had too much to do. Other times she would ask me help her brothers with their homework when they had questions or math problems before I returned home. Her two little sisters were too young to go to school, but her neighbors (Weiwei called them aunties and grandmas) were taking care of them in turns when her father had to leave for work and Weiwei had to go to school.

Our school building was a separate two-storey building on the factory grounds. There were two other buildings, one for sales and one for administration and storage. The factory was about half a mile away. We went to school in the mornings and ate lunch at school and then we walked to the factory where we worked all afternoon.

The first floor of our building was mainly for school administration and teaching staff. There were three classrooms and a ping pong room on the second floor. We had 25 students in our class. There was another class of about 25 students who had enrolled a year earlier.

We studied Chinese, math, English, history, and politics from eight o'clock until noon; then we spent afternoons learning work skills and working on different job assignments at the factory. Most of my classmates were assigned to work on looms weaving sweater pieces or on sewing machines sewing the sweater pieces together. My classmate Xiufang and I were assigned to work in the Technical Department learning how to draw sweater patterns with detailed specifications and instructions on stencil paper , which we then reproduced on a mimeograph machine to distribute to the workers who operated the looms and wove the sweaters.

It was an important job and was not easy to learn at first. We had to use even pressure to write and draw on the stencil paper with a sharp steel pen on top of a steel board. Then we moved the stencil paper around to fit the steel board to complete the drawing and copy all the specifications and production instructions. When this was done, our supervisor or technician would proofread the whole thing.

If there were only one or two small errors, we could fix it by applying a special liquid, let it dry, and then rewrite on top of the mistakes. But if there were too many mistakes, we had to redo the whole thing. It was a very detailed job and we had to be able to focus all our attention for several hours on the job. I actually enjoyed it. I thought my experience of being the blackboard monitor in elementary school had prepared me for this kind of job. I had learned how to copy pictures and writings and how to focus for several hours on the task. I had no idea that little job in school would prepare me so well for this technical procedure.

Producing copies of the blueprint was pretty easy. We just mixed the ink very thoroughly before applying it evenly onto the copy screen which held the stencil paper. If the ink was not applied evenly, the copies would not come out clean. It would be a nightmare if we broke the stencil and the ink got all over our hands, face, and clothes.

Xiufang and I did make a mess during our first week on the job. One afternoon after we finished our drawing and writing, the technician proofread our work and said, "No errors. Good job. They are ready to go."

We thought since our supervisor was busy, we could print copies ourselves. So we applied the ink evenly and carefully and the copies came out clean, but just a little too light. We thought if we pushed a little harder on the copy screen, the copies would come out darker. So we applied more pressure on the copy screen; this caused the stencil paper to leak. We were a little worried that our supervisor would be disappointed with us. While we were trying to fix the leak problem with our fingers, we got ink all over us. Our supervisor walked into the printing room and just laughed, "Are you girls trying to take an ink bath?" We explained the situation and apologized. He looked carefully at the stencil paper, "Since you haven't applied enough ink, I think we can fix the problem. Go clean up and I will show you how." This was the only time we made a mess.

During these years, I was not challenged academically. School work was easy for me so I usually finished all my homework during lunch break or by the second break in the afternoon. But I learned about life, people, and work habits at this school.

There was a little pond by the school building where I often sat with my friends under the long branches of a willow tree to eat my lunch. Lunch always consisted of two ounces of steamed bun or rice and a bowl of clear vegetable soup. Some of my classmates would run as quickly as they could after class to be the first in the soup line so they could get bits of vegetables and potatoes from the bottom of the soup container. These bits were usually gone when I got there, but I consoled myself with the fact that the soup was free. I used my ration coupons carefully to last me the whole month. At first, some of the boys in my class would use up their coupons in two weeks and would end up without bun or rice coupons for the next two weeks. Eventually they learned how to ration themselves to two ounces of steamed bun or rice a day.

By the second year, I had made more friends among my classmates, so my studies and work became more enjoyable and fun. We visited each other's homes and got to know each other better. Xiufang became another good friend. Since we worked at the same department and had the same supervisor, we spent a lot of time together at work and after hours. We visited each other's families and offered whatever treats we had at home, even though we had next to nothing to offer. A cup of tea and some rice sesame balls if we were lucky. Otherwise just a cup of tea would be fine.

From this exposure outside the circle of my family and my little neighborhood, I discovered that people were basically kind and generous by nature and they were willing to help each other when necessary. They were as hospitable as their circumstances allowed.

While I stepped a little outside the circle of my family and neighborhood, my older brother Youfu took a great leap into the frontier 2500 miles away. In 1963, when Youfu turned 17, he volunteered to go to Xinjiang Province to participate in the building of the frontier of our country. Xinjiang is more than 2500 miles northwest of Shanghai, close to the Russian border and was quite remote and undeveloped at that time.

Youfu chose to go because he was young, idealistic, and patriotic and had been influenced by Party propaganda calling for young people to go out west. This was three years before all youth in China's cities were sent to work in the countryside or in factories when the Cultural Revolution was officially launched in 1966.

Youfu knew that our parents wouldn't agree to his decision to go to Xinjiang because he was the oldest son. So one day, without asking, he took the family registration book from the top drawer of our dresser in the attic. The local police issued every family a registration book and all family members' names, births, deaths and residence status were recorded in this book, which one had to produce to do anything official in Communist China. Youfu needed the registration book in order to apply to go to the frontier.

With the registration book in his hand, Youfu went to the Neighborhood Committee and said that he wanted to go where he was most needed. There was a prevailing belief that the further you were away from home, the closer you were to the teachings of the great leader Chairman Mao. It all sounded very glorious on the surface and very attractive to an inexperienced and impressionable young man. My parents had hoped that Youfu would be able to work in Shanghai and help them support our large family. Once he was registered and his name was on the list of young people going to the frontier, they could do nothing to stop him.

The neighborhood committee team came to our home, beating drums and gongs and carrying a red poster with gold characters stating: "Congratulations Youfu Shen for your proletarian patriotism to build the frontier of our great

Motherland." They stopped at our house, attracting quite a few neighbors, and pasted the banner to the center of our front door for all to see. There were two other families whose sons had also volunteered, and they had red posters on their doors, too. One of the committee members congratulated our parents for producing a young man with such patriotic spirit. As soon as they left, my mother closed the door and cried in the kitchen while Youfu was saying good-bye to his friends and our neighbors outside.

My mother cried every day after Youfu left, and I remember that she often got up in the middle of the night because she couldn't sleep. Youfu was her firstborn surviving son, and now he was so far away from home. Her eyes were always red with tears, and she frequently used her handkerchief to wipe them. She did this so often that her eyes were red and swollen and she couldn't even see things clearly enough to sew.

All the years we were growing up, my mother made everything we wore by hand, from underwear to cotton shoes. She never wasted anything and saved every scrap of worn clothing and material. Since she did not have a sewing machine, the sewing was all done by hand; we girls helped her sew, knit, crochet and embroider. We knitted and crocheted hats, gloves, socks, sweaters and sewed blouses, shirts, jackets and pants all by hand. She even showed us how to tailor clothes and embroider pillowcases and bed linens. We were all seamstresses for the family.

The hardest job was to sew the bottoms of the cotton shoes. My mother would glue layer after layer of cotton strips (little pieces of old, worn-out cloth) onto a piece of heavy new cloth to make the bottom soles of the shoes. Then she would air the piece in the sun for a few days before cutting it to fit each person's feet.

My elder brother Youfu and I helped her sew the bottom soles of the shoes. We used a big needle and strong thread. The bottoms of the shoes were usually from half an inch to one inch thick according to the age of the person who would wear the shoes. It was not easy to force the needle through the many thick, hard, layers of cloth comprising each shoe sole. Youfu and I broke quite a few needles as we learned. But every day, we did a few stitches here and a few stitches there after school so my mother's hands would not be sore at the end of each day. We usually made two pairs of shoes every year for each family member, one pair for the winter season and the other pair for spring and summer. We had eight in our family, so we made 16 pairs of shoes annually. In difficult times, we still managed to make six pairs of shoes for six children. The winter new shoes were distributed on New Year's Eve to each family member.

My mother was always thinking about the least expensive and most efficient way to accomplish any task. She taught us, "When you do any job, pay attention to what you are doing. Try not to hurry, otherwise you might have to do the job twice. Thus, you will waste a lot of time. Think ahead for the next thing you will do, and find the best approach to get the job done well. This applies to every task including your school work."

Every Chinese Spring Festival, all the children in China were expected to receive at least one new jacket and one new pair of shoes for the holidays. Even in the most difficult times, my mother did not break this tradition, as all of us badly needed the clothes she made for us each year. Most of the other clothes we wore were hand-me-downs, so a new jacket and a pair of new shoes were the basic items she needed to provide for each child for the New Year.

Mother never had enough new fabrics. But she figured out ways to use her old clothes and the older children's outgrown clothes to make new jackets for the younger children. She turned the inside of the old fabric out so that the new clothes she made appeared to be nice. We were always very happy to wear our repurposed jackets and new shoes she gave us for the New Year. But I knew how many days and nights my mother had worked to finish six new jackets and six new pairs of shoes for us by the Chinese New Year.

After Youfu left, Mother developed an eye inflammation from crying and wiping her eyes so often. My Dad had to beg her to see a doctor. She finally agreed to go. I went with her to the local clinic and got her some medicine and eye drops.

At the same time, I also had to find a way to help my mother get over her sadness and depression, even though I missed Youfu very much myself. I knew one way to cheer her up was to sing songs we learned at school. So we girls sang together whenever we had time, such as before dinner, after we finished our homework and on Sunday afternoons. When we sewed and embroidered together, I also started to sing Shaoxing opera from my parents' hometown, which I knew both of my parents loved. Even our youngest brother Youfa, who was about five then, could sing some parts of the Shaoxing Opera in his funny way, which made our mother laugh.

Since I became the eldest child in the home after Youfu left, I had to take care of my mother and help her with everyday household duties in addition to all the chores Youfu and I had done together. In other words, I felt like I was left holding the bag for Youfu. I admired Youfu for his courage to go to the frontier. But at the same time, I resented him for doing this to our parents, especially to our mother, and to our whole family when we all needed him at home.

Dad tried to be cheerful when he got home from work, but I could tell he missed Youfu, too. He did not sing Shaoxing opera as he used to after work while holding the young ones on his lap. Youfu's leaving deeply impacted us all. If there was a silver lining, it was the impact it had on my second brother Yougen. He became a great help during this time. He started to do more of the chores Youfu used to do outside the house and to help our Dad with the men's work, such as building shelves in the backyard and repairing the bamboo chair and stool legs.

We tried not to mention Youfu's name so Mother wouldn't cry, but we didn't stop missing him until he finally came home for a two-week visit three years later in 1966. After that, he came home every year and spent his two-week annual vacation with us in Shanghai.

My elder brother's choice to follow the government's call to the frontier was very hard on my family at the time. Even though we both resented and admired Youfu when he left our family to follow his dream, I believe he set a good example for us; he showed us that one acceptable alternative was to put the needs of the country above even those of the family.

We all learned how to work hard and efficiently from our parents. Once we were 17 and had graduated from middle school, we were ready to jump into a larger world, each in our own way.

In retrospect, I believe I made the right decision for myself when I listened to my parents' advice to go to the Industrial Middle School instead of going to a regular middle school. Had I placed my own wish, my own dream, before my family's needs, it would have been for personal, not patriotic, reasons. With such a selfish attitude, I might have been caught up in the movement of "going up to the mountains and down to the countryside" like so many young people were during the Cultural Revolution. If I had done that, who knows what would have become of me? As it was, things worked out all right for me in the end. In the years to come, quite unexpectedly, right in the middle of the turbulent times of the Cultural Revolution, almost like a miracle, I would get another chance to keep my dream of becoming a teacher alive.

Youfeng Shen

5 – Turbulent Years
1965-1976

By mid-1965 Mao had gradually regained control of the Communist Party with the support of Lin Biao, the new defense minister. During the seesaw struggle between Mao and the Government leadership under Liu Shaoqi, Mao decided to break through the Marxist-Leninist framework itself and destroy the Party whose loyalty he could no longer command. Mao declared that the Soviet Union, the first socialist country in the world, had deviated from the Marxist-Leninist principles, turned revisionist and betrayed the cause of Communism. He warned that China must not make the same mistake. The only way to keep China on the right track towards Communism was to launch the Great Proletarian Cultural Revolution.

Mao further pointed out that "Those representatives of the bourgeoisie who have sneaked into the Party, the government, the army and various spheres of culture are a bunch of counter-revolutionary revisionists". Mao alleged that bourgeois elements had infiltrated the government and society at large. He wanted to eliminate his rivals within the Communist Party. Backed by Lin Biao, Mao used the fervor, ignorance and idealism of the high school and college students of China to create the Red Guards. He further pointed out that "Rebellion against reactionaries is justified". After this Red Guard groups spread all over China.

Initially the Red Guards were concentrated in Beijing. The early groups of Red Guards were mainly high officials' children. They were indoctrinated to target and denounce "capitalist-roaders" (anyone who was in power and favored capitalism in even the smallest way) and the "five black categories" (landlords, rich peasants, counter-revolutionaries, bad elements and rightists) and to destroy the "four Olds" (old customs, old culture, old habits, and old ideas.) All schools closed down and ceased functioning as educational institutions. Instead, they were used mainly to brainwash the youth with Chairman Mao's Little Red Book, Quotations of Chairman Mao. Political meetings and "struggle" meetings to criticize "capitalist-roaders" and "the five black categories" were held in schools, factories, and, eventually, everywhere in China.

Groups of Red Guards traveled from Beijing to all the major cities of China and roamed the streets looking for victims. I saw groups from Beijing helping local groups of Red Guards in Shanghai in their mad quest for victims. They raided people's homes, destroyed antiques, tore up paintings and works of art. Bonfires were lit in the street swallowing up books, musical instruments, pictures or anything old and valuable. Even some of the museums, temples, ancient tombs, pagodas and churches were either vandalized or destroyed. Quite a few teachers, writers, professors, and artists committed suicide after being beaten and humiliated by their own students and colleagues. These were people who supported the practical policies of Liu Shaoqi within the Communist Party and were the original political targets of Mao and his Cultural Revolution. I was told that one prominent professor at the Shanghai Conservatory of Music jumped from his office windows and died instantly after he had seen his music books and his life-long collections being destroyed and burned to ashes.

Others in Mao's faction, running the Cultural Revolution for him, used it for their own ends and kept Mao uninformed of their activities. This was especially true of the infamous "Gang of Four" which held control of the Party from the beginning of the Cultural Revolution in 1966 until Mao Zedong's death in 1976. These four included Jiang Qing, Mao's wife, a member of the Central Politburo during the Cultural Revolution; Zhang Chunqiao, a vice-premier of the People's Republic and a leading Marxist theoretician; Yao Wenyuan, also a vice premier and a political critic of literature; and Wang Hongwen, a former Shanghai worker and a vice-chairman of the Communist Party.

These four highly-placed and powerful individuals were ambitious and believed any means were justified to achieve their own political ends. They were responsible for the deaths of many innocent Chinese citizens. In October 1976, after Mao's death, the "Gang of Four" were deposed and brought before the Chinese courts to answer for their crimes against the people during the preceding 10 years. All of them and their minions ended up in prison. But during their reign, from 1966 to 1976, the only safety for most Chinese citizens was in being an invisible "worker," "peasant" or "soldier."

My elementary school teacher, Mrs. Zheng, was criticized and humiliated by Red Guards from her school because she was from a rich family and she had relatives living abroad. After she was humiliated by her students and colleagues, the Shanghai Red Guards raided her house. Some of her old books, antiques and valuable Chinese paintings and works of calligraphy were confiscated. Many years later, when I visited her during one of my trips home, she told me that all her paintings were returned; because unlike Beijing Red Guards, Shanghai Red Guards kept a list of the items they took and gave them back to her when Deng Xiaoping was in power in the early 1980s.

With everything going on around us, our parents told us not to join the Red Guards and to stay away from them, especially the Red Guards from Beijing. We could tell the difference in their manners. Beijing Red Guards tended to be haughty, louder, and more violent. We were instructed to be careful of everything we said or did at all times. As a result, we stayed close to home, and we did not join the Red Guards. We trusted no one outside home and talked to no one except our parents.

The only exception in our family was my second brother Yougen who joined the Red Guards in his school at age 14. He followed Mao's instructions instead of our parents'; and he also followed the lead of his so called "friends." We did not know why Yougen wanted to join the Red Guards, except that he thought he was answering Chairman Mao's call and that he was joining the "revolution." As a middle child, I think Yougen was a little neglected in some ways. So when school closed down, he had nothing else to do but join the Red Guards with his friends.

The Red Guards closely monitored the daily lives of persons labeled as "capitalist roaders" or members of the "five black categories" in our neighborhood. There were about four to five of these unfortunate people in our neighborhood. Mrs. Wang, the elementary school principal who lived in House No. 11, was one of them.

Mrs. Wang was from a landlord's family, but she had been in charge of the local elementary school for a long time. She was labeled by Red Guards as a "capitalist roader" who followed Liu Shaoqi's education guidelines. During a "struggle" meeting they accused her of being an American spy because one of her brothers was living in the United States. They also accused her of being a "counter-revolutionary". She was forced to wear a big paper hat which read: "Niu gui she shen" (the monsters and freaks, the enemy of the people) which was a general term for all sorts of "bad elements" during the Cultural Revolution.

I watched these unfortunate people with apprehension and could not understand why Mrs. Wang, an educated and professional woman, should be humiliated like this. Mrs. Wang was a good principal and a wonderful mother. She did not deserve this kind of treatment.

Every morning, these four and sometimes five unfortunate neighbors were lined up in the middle of our courtyard with their heads down to receive daily "orders" from the Red Guards. They were assigned to sweep the neighborhood streets and clean public places. My brother and his associates monitored them and checked their work and then gave them more orders for the day. Some of them were sent home to "write their confessions"; some were sent to different struggle meetings in schools, factories or their work units.

After a few weeks, I did not see Mrs. Wang, so I asked Yougen where she was. He told me that she was locked up in a place called "cow-sheds" because of her stubbornness and bad attitude towards the Red Guards.

I didn't understand why Yougen had joined the Red Guards instead of listening to our parents. Mrs. Wang had always been kind to her neighbors and her students; how could Yougen stoop so low as to humiliate such a fine woman? Sometimes he even pushed these unfortunate people around to make them "confess" He emulated the Red Guards from Beijing and some of his friends. When he was younger, Yougen used to listen to our parents, but he changed during the Cultural Revolution. Being a teenager, he was brainwashed and wanted to be a "big shot".

I argued with him, asking him how he could be so mean as to push his own school principal's head down when he knew how well she had treated him and all of her students. He just ignored me. He was blindly and impulsively following his own adolescent ignorance and the behaviors of the other Red Guards.

The people of my generation were brought up to worship Chairman Mao. In 1966, Mao issued a proclamation that all young people who wished to see him could travel to Beijing to do so. He also ordered that all young people should have the chance to see the real world and that all local governments must welcome and provide services for such traveling youths. Consequently, millions of young people traveled to every corner of China for free. Wherever they went, free meals, transportation, and shelter were provided at local government expense. All trains and public buses had to transport them for free. Most of the students and teenagers took this opportunity to travel all over the country extensively.

When Yougen heard this, he was excited. He traveled to Hunan Province to visit Chairman Mao's birthplace with some of his friends. He planned to continue on and see our elder brother Youfu in Xinjiang Province 2500 miles away. However, he waited too long, and the free travel program was terminated, so he had to return home.

Silently, we watched him clean himself up after his trip. He received a lot of criticism from his family and friends after getting back. The kids in the neighborhood often called him a "boss" or a "big shot". My father had a serious talk with him after he returned from his trip. A couple of months later, Yougen finally quit the Red Guards. I believe my father saved Yougen from his youthful foolishness. Yougen's friends did not try to retaliate against him when he quit the Red Guards because they all respected our father as a "no-nonsense" man. After a while, some of Yougen's friends followed his example and also quit the Red Guards.

In 1969 when he was 17, Yougen was sent to work as a peasant on a commune in Jiangxi province in the so-called "going up to the mountains and down to the countryside" movement. After nearly two years' hard work on the commune, Yougen joined the People's Liberation Army in winter 1970. He served in the Army for over four years. Then in 1975 he returned to Jiangxi province and found employment as a security officer with a big oil company in Nanchang.

All in all, my brother Yougen created quite a stir in our family with his brief excursion into the Red Guards. Like many youths who were duped into this experience by unscrupulous politicians, I think he later came to regret the impulsiveness of his youth. He has since matured into a responsible adult and a loving member of our family.

Our father's refusal to become involved in politics and in the Communist Party and his status as a Model Master Worker of his factory saved us all during these dangerous political upheavals.

Both my parents were extremely careful, hardworking people. In addition to all the work and responsibilities Mother had for our family, she sometimes took in wash and sewing for other people from which she earned about 10 yuan a month. On many occasions, our father received the Model Master Worker awards at his factory, which usually included household items such as thermos bottles, wash towels and basins, or sometimes a monetary bonus. The Party Secretary at his factory tried to persuade him to join the Communist Party many times, but my father always politely refused.

Dad told the Party Secretary, "I appreciate your asking, but I have a wife and six children to support. I also have my in-laws in Shaoxing to support. They all rely on me. I cannot afford the membership fees, and I don't have any time for the Party responsibilities and meetings. Working hard for my country and my family is all I can handle right now." Dad was not only a Model Master Worker, but also was a master of discretion.

I remember another important thing that my father did which probably saved all of us from the political movement and upheavals as well as the Cultural Revolution. My mother used to run a "lao Hu-zhao" (Tiger Stove) which sold hot water in the neighborhood. Just before the San Fan (three anti) and Wu Fan (five anti) movements between 1951 and 1952, my father made a decision to close down the store.

When my mother was running the hot water store, all our neighbors were customers and they called her "Lao Ban Niang" (Woman Boss.) If my dad had not made the decision to close the store when he did, my mother might have been labeled as a "small capitalist" by our neighborhood committee, and our family could have suffered during all the political movements and the Cultural Revolution. Mother might have been sent away to a labor camp for a few years or even longer. This would have caused our family extreme hardship and devastating consequences.

As I am writing now and thinking about my father, I miss him so much. Dad was an intelligent man, a good husband, and a wonderful father. He was always happy and contented even in the most difficult situations. He loved his life and family to the fullest and was always kind and thoughtful towards his family, friends, co-workers, and neighbors.

I remember when we were young, he used to let one of us sit around his neck while holding two older children's hands when we went out. He was very protective, and did what he thought was best for the family. He saved our family from persecution during the long years of political upheaval occurring all around us while we were growing up.

I love him and hold him dearly in my heart. I never got to say this to him when he was alive. It was not our custom to express our feelings in this way, but now I wish I had been able to tell him how much I loved him. I am grateful that in later years

I was able to go back to China and spend some time with him before his death. He died in 1994 at the age of 86, having lived a full life and having successfully shepherded his wife and six children through turbulent times. Even throughout the 10 years of devastation during the Cultural Revolution, my father's solid Master Worker status and his sound judgement kept us inconspicuous enough to stave off danger.

But the same cannot be said for another branch of our extended family. My paternal great aunt (my grandma Shen's twin sister), who was married to an industrialist in Shanghai, was not so fortunate. She did not survive the Cultural Revolution.

Her husband owned a couple of factories in the Hongkou District. He died in the early 1950s just after the Communist Party confiscated his factories. During the Cultural Revolution, the Red Guards confiscated most of my great aunt's remaining valuable belongings such as paintings, antiques, some old books and furniture. Because her younger son once complained about the Communist Party's confiscation of his family property, he was labeled as an "anti-party, anti-social rightist" during the Anti-Rightist Movement in 1957 and was sent to a labor camp for "reformation". When he was released a few years later, he went back to work in his father's confiscated factory. He became a very quiet and cautious man.

Before the Cultural Revolution, I used to spend one week every summer at my great aunt's big apartment by the Huangpu River in a wealthy neighborhood of Shanghai. She was in her 60s when I last knew her, and I remember her as an elegant, lonely, old lady who missed her husband and her lost fortune. I was between eight and 14 years old when I used to visit her. My

Dad would take me across town by an electric tram on Sunday, his only day off. He would spend some time with her and her son's family and then leave me there with her. The following Sunday, he would come and pick me up.

When I went to visit her, I loved to watch the huge ocean going ships from her balcony as they sailed up and down the Huangpu River. I often wondered where all these big ships had been and where they were going next.

My great aunt lived near the old European Bund called "Wai Tan", which was the waterfront area in central Shanghai. It was within the former International Settlement, established in 1863 after the British and American settlements were formally united. Along the area by the river stood skyscrapers, buildings of Western style dating back to the early 19th century. To walk along the Bund in the summer morning with my great aunt when I was a child was a fun and exciting experience. The street was always alive with noise and movement. Horns, whistles, the cries of peddlers selling rice balls and spring rolls and the music of Chi Gong practice in the public park all became a vivid, unique and harmonious picture in my mind. There was a public park which we always passed by on the way to the Bund. One day my great aunt stopped at the entrance and told me that years ago the park had been posted with a sign that said "No dogs and Chinese allowed". I could not understand how we Chinese were not allowed in the park while foreigners were. This was our territory after all. My great aunt held my hand and said, "Just be glad we can enter the park anytime we want now." During my research, I found that some scholars disputed the existence of the sign, but it was apparently a story that a lot of people including my great aunt believed happened. The oppression, discrimination, and humiliation that the sign signifies were certainly real.

After walking around the Bund for about half an hour, my great aunt usually got tired; she would sit on a bench to rest her feet while I played and watched the comings and goings of the people and all the activities around me. Sometimes she would buy me some sesame rice balls, and other times she would get a big bowl of wonton soup and some crispy spring rolls to take home for our snack in the mid-day. Then she would call a rickshaw to take us back to her house with our still warm and delicious snack.

At night, I slept with my great aunt in her huge redwood bed with drawers all around three sides of the bedframe. Sometimes she would ask me to open the left bottom drawer which contained all kinds of candy and chocolates or the right bottom drawer which held cookies and biscuits. She told me to take whatever I liked. Munching food in her bed and listening to her stories, I thought I was in heaven.

At home we were lucky just to get enough to eat each day to stave off our hunger. There were no luxuries except at my great aunt's house. Even so, after a week's stay with her I was always glad to go home. She always wrapped me a bag of goodies to take home to share with my siblings.

When I was with her, I noticed that her two sons seldom visited. Even when they did, they didn't say much. In her big and fancy home, there was no noise, no laughter at all. She was unhappy most of the time, so I began to get depressed by the end of the week. She would stare at her dead husband's portrait and cry if I were not there to talk with her. I learned how to divert her attention to the noise and ocean-going ships outside her windows. I asked her a lot of questions so that she had to return to reality and answer my questions.

My great aunt told me that when they first arrived in Shanghai in the early 1920s, her husband was not rich. When I was growing up, I often heard people say "Shanghai is the Paradise for Adventurers", and that was true for my great uncle. He hit it big in the Shanghai textile industry in the 1930s, eventually owning two factories and two clothing stores. He produced fabrics in his factories and sold them retail and made clothing in his clothing stores.

In the 1930s, the metropolis of Shanghai absorbed all kinds of people. Shanghai took foreigners and strangers at face value, believed what they said, never asked for a passport or visa. This westernized city rejected no one, not even the peasant fleeing his flooded home and ravaged fields to make a pittance in the factories (like my father when he was 15) or to beg in the street. Shanghai rejected neither the White Russians who fled from the revolution and civil war nor the Jewish refugees from Hitler's Europe to whom the rest of the world had shut its doors. Even the underground Chinese communists with prices on their heads found Shanghai a safe hiding place, not to mention an international assortment of criminals and fugitives from justice who found this "Paradise for the Adventurers" a comfortable spot in which to hide and lie low. This was the time when my great uncle made his money. He became a very slick and quite successful entrepreneur in Shanghai.

My great aunt once asked my father to work for her husband in his factories; they certainly could have used my father's skills as a dye-master. But my father did not want to complicate the family relationship. His response was that he was happy with his job, and he liked to live in the Xuhui District where the cost of living was cheaper and schools were better for the children. My mother did not want to move either. I really think my parents made a smart decision. Otherwise, we probably would have been caught up in the Cultural Revolution due to the close connection with my great aunt's family.

Our great aunt never came to our house; she was careful not to stigmatize us by letting our neighbors know that we had a wealthy relative. My great aunt was always sweet and kind to us even though we were her poor relatives. She cared and loved us in her special way, and we loved her back dearly in our special and silent way. I was too young to remember much of my own grandma Shen who died when I was only six; but I remember her twin sister, my great aunt, more vividly than my other siblings do, as I was the only child who had spent a week each summer for eight years with her before the Cultural Revolution in 1966.

We usually saw her again during the Chinese New Year when she invited us to her house or a restaurant to celebrate the New Year together. After the dinner, she usually gave each of us a red envelope containing "lucky money". We thanked her and then gave the red envelopes to our mother to keep. Mother later used that money to help pay for our tuition and school supplies.

At an early age, I learned through my great aunt that money is not what makes people happy. I observed that my family never had enough money, but we were always happy. My great aunt always had lots of money, but she was not happy. She had lost her husband forever and her younger son for a few years to a political movement. All the money she had and all the nice things in her home could not replace these losses.

Her older son had never married. He was an accountant in a big company and kept a low profile by following the "trend of the masses" just as my father had done. My great aunt also had one daughter who had married and had gone to Hong Kong long before the Cultural Revolution. I have seen her pictures. She did not have any contact with her mother.

Unfortunately, we had to curtail our contact with this branch of the family to avoid scrutiny by the Red Guards during the Cultural Revolution. Because we couldn't contact my great aunt and her family during that time, we didn't know what had happened to her. We only learned about her death from her oldest son a few years after the Cultural Revolution had ended. She died in her sleep at 75 with a broken heart. This was very sad news for me, as I had always loved my great aunt. She was an unwitting victim of the political movement and the Great Proletarian Cultural Revolution.

Youfeng Shen

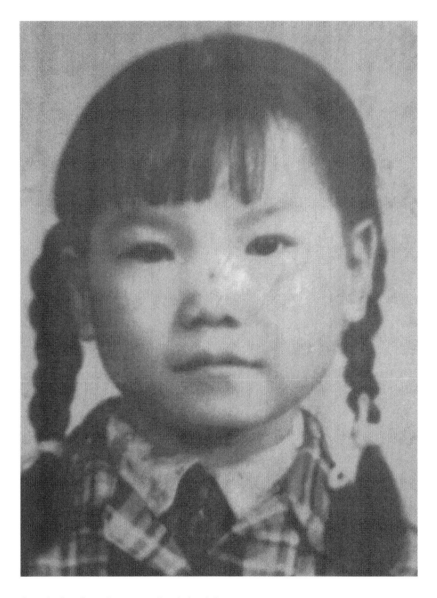

Age 6, the day of my grandma's burial.

My elder brother Youfu volunteered to go to the Western
Frontier at age 17, in 1963.

Age 17, I worked as a lab apprentice in the textile factory.

Family photo taken in 1966 when Youfu visited home after 3 years at the frontier. He was the 1st on the right.

Folkstone School of English Studies in England, 1970. The Principal, Mr. O'Connel, was the 5th from the left, front row. I was the 1st from the left, 2nd row.

Family photo, 1989, a few years before I left for America.

Mother and Daughter, 1997. Xiao Bo joined me from college
for winter break.

6 – Work and Courtship
1965-1970

While the pre-Cultural Revolution tensions were building up in Beijing, our everyday life in Shanghai was still normal. After I graduated from the Industrial Middle School in June 1965, I looked forward to spending some time with my friends and helping Mama finish her six pairs of home-made cotton shoes.

In early August, three months before my 17th birthday, I received a letter from the Shanghai Textile Labor Committee informing me that I was assigned to work as an apprentice at Shanghai No. 12 Woolen Textile Factory. My parents and I were excited about this news as I was going to be able to support myself and help my family.

This Factory was about three times the size of No. 8 Sweater Factory and employed over 2000 workers. It operated 24 hours a day, seven days a week and had all kinds of textile machinery running day and night.

When I reported to work in the middle of August, it was the hottest time of the year in Shanghai. Eight young people my age waited on the bench of the Personnel Office that morning. We began our three-day orientation at eight o'clock. After we all sat down around a big rectangular table, a middle-aged man, Xia Zhuren (Director Xia), came out of his office and greeted us. We all introduced ourselves and he made a short welcome speech. Then he introduced us to his assistant, Miss Lin who was in her mid-20s. He looked at his watch and said, "I have another meeting to attend. Miss Lin will show you around the factory and take care of you today. Tomorrow you will meet your department head and supervisor and learn about your jobs. On your third day, you will meet your master worker who will take you to your individual department and meet the rest of the people you are going to work with."

Director Xia was very businesslike and left in a hurry. We followed Miss Lin to a huge warehouse where all kinds of wool fabric were stacked as high as a two-story building. Miss Lin gathered us around her and pointed to the next building, "We just passed our warehouse which is our main storage building. But this building in front of you is where our operation starts. In our textile industry, scouring is the first important step."

"What is scouring?" one of the young men asked.

"Scouring is the washing and cleaning of raw wool material and removing any foreign material such as sand, dirt, grease, and so forth," Miss Lin replied and led us into the building.

As soon as we entered the building, we sniffed some kind of smell from some big machines. Miss Lin continued, "The wool is scoured in a series of alkaline baths with water, soap and soda ash. Then the rollers in the scouring machine squeeze the excess water from the fleece."

A few young workers waved at Miss Lin, and one older worker came over and asked Miss Lin, "Are we getting some new blood?"

Miss Lin responded to him quietly, "I am not sure, but we should know by tomorrow."

Next we followed her through a concrete basketball court to an old two-story building. We went upstairs to the Carding Department where the wool passed through a series of metal teeth that disentangled, cleaned and blended the fibers into a continuous web ready for spinning. I noticed some middle-aged women were operating their machines while wearing white cotton aprons and white cotton caps over their heads to prevent floating fabric sticking onto their hair. Since it was pretty noisy, we didn't ask any questions. It was clear this was the second stage in the process.

Then we followed Miss Lin to an overpass connecting the old building with a new building. She raised her arm and motioned us to stop. "We just toured our two workshops. We are going to have our lunch break for about an hour since it is your first day and you may need more time to know where you are. Usually we only break for half an hour. The dining hall is on the first floor of the new building. I will meet you all here again at twelve sharp."

After lunch break Miss Lin showed us three more workshops. First, we toured the Spinning Department where spinning frames produced threads or yarn from wool fibers at a very fast speed. Then we stopped at the Weaving Department where rows of young women were working on their long weaving looms. Most of them looked like they were in their late teens or early 20s. These long looms were running at a pretty fast rhythm while the young workers ran around the looms troubleshooting any problems occurring. It seemed they were operating on several machines at the same time. They were required to wear white aprons and white cotton caps while working.

The last place we toured was the Dyeing Department where some male workers were operating rotary dyeing machines. I saw some female workers were stirring dyes into some big, round containers. There were stacks of whitish grey wool fabrics by the big, round containers ready to be put into the containers to be soaked with dyes of different colors. It was all new and exciting to me.

On our second day, we met our department heads and supervisors and received our assignments. We read our job descriptions, rules and regulations of the factory and our responsibilities carefully. We were encouraged to ask any questions we had, and all the questions were answered by our supervisor or department head.

On our last day of orientation, we were introduced to our master workers and went to our individual department to meet our team members. It seemed that every department needed some new employees (who they called "new blood") and had requested more apprentices. Of the eight apprentices, five were females and only three were males. Two girls were assigned to the spinning department, another two were assigned to the weaving department and I was assigned to the chemical lab. Of the three young men, one would learn to be a beamer (who would be responsible for moving beams of yarn around) as he was tall and strong, one would go to the scouring department, and the last young man would learn how to be a mechanic to repair machines.

Later, my supervisor told me that I was assigned to be an apprentice in the chemical laboratory where I would learn how to blend dyes to color woolen materials as my father had done for cotton fabrics. My father was well-known in the local textile industry for his skills. They thought it would be a good fit for me to do the lab work.

My supervisor was a veteran of the Korean War and was in charge of our laboratory. Her name was Pinhua Zhang, but we all called her "Zhang Lao Shi" (Teacher Zhang) to show our respect. She volunteered in the Korean War when she was a student from 1950 to 1953. After the war, she completed her college and started to work as a lab technician and supervisor. She was in her late 30s and was very lean and athletic with short bobbed hair.

My Master Worker's name was Shueilian Ju. I called her "Ju Shi Fu" (Master Worker Ju). A Master Worker was your mentor, trainer and immediate supervisor and was a very important person in your life. She was in her early 40s, and she had two young daughters aged five and three. She was always busy, in a hurry, trying to do three things at once. But she was very patient with me and with my questions.

I was paid 18 yuan a month (about three U.S. dollars) as a new apprentice. By saving most of my money for about six months, I was able to purchase my first brand new bicycle. I never owned anything so expensive before, but my parents insisted that I needed a reliable bicycle to get to work on time. I felt independent, self-sufficient and happy. Now I could ride to anywhere in the city on my new bike.

During the first week I rode my new bike to work, my neighbor, who I called Big Sister, told me to follow her while she led the way through the busy traffic. She worked as an accountant at another textile factory very close to my factory. After following her for a week, I felt comfortable to ride by myself, but she still checked on me now and then.

The distance from my home to the factory was about 10 miles, approximately a 30-minute ride on my bike. Every morning I got up early and joined the crowd of bicyclists negotiating my way to work through busy morning traffic. After a few months, I decided to try to find a better route to work. I studied the Shanghai map carefully and found a straighter route with less traffic. In some parts of the city, there were big, tall sycamore trees lined up like huge umbrellas on both sides of the street protecting people from rain and sun. It made my heart sing when I passed through these streets. When I told Big Sister what I had found, she joined me next day and said, "You are such a smart girl. I have been riding the same route for 12 years, and you have found a better way to work in just a few months."

Our factory was one of many textile factories in the Pu Tuo District, which was famous for producing high quality woolen textile products for export. My Master Worker, Ju Shi Fu, was a tall, plump woman with soft, brownish shoulder-length hair. Even though she was always on the run, she never failed to say to me every morning, "Xiao Shen, I am happy to see you with your big smile. You have brought your energy and sunshine to our little lab." I was really happy and felt grown up and independent. I enjoyed working with her and the other women in our lab.

It was not long before Ju Shi Fu and I became good friends. She invited me to her home one Sunday afternoon, and I met her two daughters. Then I invited her to visit my family. My parents liked Ju Shi Fu very much. My mother even offered to take care of her two daughters when she needed help. She readily accepted. Her two little girls loved to come to our home even though we didn't have any toys for them. But they brought their own dolls and played hide and seek in our attic. They called my mother "Grandma" and me "Auntie." This was the first time someone had called me "Auntie"; at 17 I felt honored and pleased with this new title.

Ju Shi Fu was like my extended family and her two young daughters became very close to my whole family as well. Later, when I needed a place to stay in Beijing after coming back from England, Ju arranged for me to stay with her younger sister, who worked as a researcher at the Beijing Academy of Agricultural Science.

Ju Shi Fu's husband worked in Xian which was over 850 miles north of Shanghai. He could only come home to see her and the children once a year on his annual two-week vacation, so she was practically a single mother. This was true at that time for many couples in China who were separated by their jobs and could not live together. Most jobs were assigned by the government according to the government's needs and quotas at the time. All personal needs were ignored. People were supposed to accept jobs and positions without second thought, putting the country's needs and government's needs before their own.

Many couples like Mr. and Mrs. Ju were separated for many years and sometimes until their retirement. The only way this could be changed was if a family emergency occurred, and you were lucky enough to be reassigned to a job near your family. Or if you had "connections", you could bribe your way through "Hou men" (the back door) to get a reassignment from a party official. Also through official channels, some couples could find a "dui diao" (matching transfer)—a person in your city of destination with the same job who wanted to transfer to the city to which you had been assigned. Most people solved this problem by using the "dui diao" method before their retirement, but it could take years before a match was found and families could be re-united.

At work, Ju Shi Fu taught me a great deal about the chemistry of textile dyes, temperature, time and processing methods. Under her guidance, I learned quickly. I enjoyed learning and experimenting with different colors on different kinds and weights of materials. I found the whole process fascinating. Usually the technical department provided our lab with specific instructions for a particular order with sample material attached. Our lab worked and experimented on small pieces of the sample material. When the target result was achieved, we then wrote down the prescription of the specific order, which included the amount of each dye color, the percentage of color combinations, the temperature, and processing time and so on. Once our prescriptions got approved by our supervisor, we sent them on to the dyeing department. The workers in the dyeing department had to follow our prescriptions exactly and apply them to large quantities of wool material.

It was a very precise and strict process, as each prescription included specifications for time, temperature, quantities of different dye colors, as well as other conditions in the dyeing process necessary to produce the correct color for that specific wool material.

Our responsibility was great, as any mistake by us could ruin a large amount of costly material. Then the whole factory would suffer. Ju Shi Fu was very strict about our accuracy in writing the prescriptions. If anyone misplaced a decimal point or wrote a wrong number, she would find it and give you a long lecture. Luckily, I had not received her long lectures because I was always careful when writing prescriptions. I double-checked, sometimes even triple-checked, everything before I sent it out. Ju Shi Fu began to trust me on details when she was busy and in a hurry.

Ju Shi Fu had two other co-workers who assisted her in the lab, and they were also amazed at my progress. In my first year I needed eight to ten tries to hit the right color percentages and combinations for certain kinds of wool material. By my second year I could target the right percentages and combinations within five to six attempts. And by my third year I was almost as good as Ju.

Ju Shi Fu and I trusted each other not only at work but also in other activities in which we were involved. We "had each other's back". One year after I started my apprenticeship, the Cultural Revolution began, and it continued for a whole decade. The Red Guards from Beijing came to Shanghai to stir up the revolution and tried to smash the Shanghai Municipal Government. Some workers from our factory and other factories nearby organized a "Workers' Team" to safeguard the Shanghai Municipal Government. Ju Shi Fu was a member of the Workers' Team. In order to support her, I joined the Workers' Team as well.

One day hundreds of workers went to Xu Hui District (very close to my home) after a day's work and sat in the offices of the municipal buildings to protect them from the Red Guards. Around midnight, a large number of Beijing Red Guards and local Red Guards from high schools and colleges rushed into the buildings. The Workers' Team tried to stop them, but they ignored us and chanted their slogan, "Zao Fan Youli! Zao Fan Youli!" (Rebellion is justified!). There were so many of them that those of us from the Workers' Team could not possibly stop them. The Red Guards outnumbered us, and they eventually took over the buildings we were trying to protect.

The leader of our Workers' Team ordered us not to fight or argue with the Red Guards but to persuade them not to do anything violent if we could. After a few hours of persuasion, there was no sign of success, so the leader in our team decided to let us all go home. There was no violence, no fighting in our part of the compound.

I remember leaving the municipal building early in the morning under the watchful eyes of a gang of Red Guards. One young man shouted at us, "Lower your head! Lower your head!" Ju Shi Fu and I held hands and left the building with our heads held up high.

Even though the Workers' Team was short-lived, this brief experience gave me a small taste of the political turmoil going on around us, and it also bound Ju and me closer than ever. When I got home that morning, my mother was waiting for me. She told me that she had been worried sick about my safety all night. She had heard from neighbors that there had been fights between Red Guards and the Workers' Team, and some workers had gotten injured. I assured her that I was with Ju Shi Fu, and we followed the order of our leader and didn't fight with the Red Guards. We just tried to persuade them and then left.

I was Ju Shi Fu's apprentice for three years until I turned almost 20. When my apprenticeship was over, I was promoted to Master Worker Shen. My pay increased from 18 yuan to 39 yuan (three yuan more than the regular worker's pay) which was a huge jump for me and big help to my family. I contributed all my pay to Mama, but she wanted me to keep half of my pay for my own expenses, as my elder brother had before me. She always told us, "Don't spend all your hard-earned money each month. Try to save half of what you have earned and put it in a bank." I started a savings account and put in 10 yuan each month. I still had nine yuan left for occasional movie tickets, books, bus fair, and going out with my girlfriends. I felt rich because I had never had pocket money before. The poverty line in China at that time was eight yuan for a person. It became my habit to save half of what I made for a rainy day or emergency until my retirement.

About a month before my three-year apprenticeship was over, the head of our factory trade union asked me privately, "Xiao Shen, do you have a boyfriend?"

"What are you saying? I thought we are not allowed to date anyone when we were an apprentice," I said and wondered why she asked me such personal questions.

"I know the policy. You are going to become a master worker next month, that's why I asked you this."

"I don't have a boyfriend."

"Well, I'd like to introduce you to a new designer in our technical department. His name is Yiren Tang, and he graduated from Sichuan University a couple of years ago. Do you know him?"

"Yes, I know him. I have talked to him a few times about some samples. He is kind of weird. Ju Shi Fu always asks me to talk to him about samples because she doesn't like him."

"You are right. He does not like Shanghai people either. But he told me that you are different. You don't have that superficial behavior the Shanghai women tend to have."

"I don't know about that. But I don't know him well enough to date him."

"He is a very smart and honest man. Why don't you give it a try? I'll arrange for you two to meet next month," she said.

I did not know what to do about her suggestion. This was the very first time anyone had talked to me about such a matter. I didn't know who to counsel with. I thought that my mother would be too old-fashioned and my sisters too young to understand, so I talked to Miss Gu, my co-worker who had become a Master Worker two years before. Miss Gu was dating an army man, and she said that 20 was a good age to start dating if I did not want to become an old maid.

Tang and I started seeing each other after work. He walked me home a few times while I pushed my bike all the way home. Then he would walk back to the factory dormitory where he lived. Usually he was the one who talked while I listened. He often seemed to criticize the government policies and factory policies as well as people he did not like. I was not comfortable with his constant negativity and opinionated behavior even though he was indeed an honest and intelligent man. He even volunteered to draw and paint Chairman Mao's portrait on the wall of our neighborhood. In fact, he did a great job and everyone in our neighborhood knew that I had a boyfriend who was a good painter. But I was afraid he might get into trouble if he was not careful.

After a few meetings with Tang, I found that we did not have much in common. We never even held hands. I was not attracted to him because he always had a sullen expression on his face and never smiled. I told our matchmaker that we did not have much in common and that I was not really ready to date anyone, so we stopped seeing each other.

From 1966 to 1970, I was on the cusp of adulthood. I was living in a contradictory and confusing world. I wanted to do my best, but at the same time I did not want to be noticed. I wanted to be pretty, but I could not afford to stand out. During the Cultural Revolution I noticed that some young women who wore pretty clothing and had long hair would come to work pretty but return home with their hair cut short and their clothing cut and ripped by the Red Guards. If pant cuffs were less than five inches wide, it was considered a "bourgeois behavior", and the Red Guards would cut the seams open to the knees.

One of the engineers in our Technical Department came to work on her bike and was stopped by some Red Guards on the street. They measured her pant cuffs and cut her cuffs open, saying they were too tight. She was a very pretty woman, and she cried when she told us about this incident. Luckily, she had a pair of extra pants at work, or she would have felt humiliated all day long wearing her mutilated pants.

While this was going on everywhere in China, all the girls in my family were limited to "safe" hair styles—pig-tails or short haircuts. Mother cut our hair. During hot summer days, she would shave Dad's and all the boys' heads.

I remember one Sunday after the haircuts, all the girls went upstairs to do some sewing with Mother. Dad was showing Youfa how to sweep hair from the cement floor, and asked the two older boys to clean the kitchen area. A neighbor came into our living area and saw the four shiny bald heads and said, "Am I in the wrong place, or has your home changed into a Buddhist temple?"

My dad responded with humor, "You want to be a monk, too? We haven't put the shaving knife away yet."

These were hard times for a young person or any person to live in if they wanted to be different from others. But we kept our humor in our family and in our little neighborhood. I was used to living in a collective environment since I was from a big family and had to share everything with my five siblings. I did what I was supposed to do as a big sister, and I felt sorry for those brave ones who defied the "normal behavior" with so-called "bourgeois behavior" and paid the price.

What really saved me were my family, my job and the books I read. Most of the books I read were borrowed from the public library. I also borrowed books from my friend's father, who was an accountant in a book store and owned some translated English classical novels including David Copperfield by Charles Dickens, Jane Eyre by Charlotte Bronte, Sister Carrie and An American Tragedy by Theodore Dreiser. As long as I was discrete and didn't tell anyone what I was reading, I could get away with reading them in the safety of my home. I also read quite a few Chinese writers, such as Lu Xun, Ba Jing, and Cao Xueqin. Chao's Dream of the Red Chamber was considered a masterpiece of Chinese literature. I read voraciously and lost myself in different places and times to escape the depressing reality around me. It worked, and I was happy being a "Shu Dai Zi" (book-worm). That was the nickname I acquired during that time.

I wanted to find someone with whom I could discuss what I had read and share my thoughts and feelings, but there was no one available. I didn't want to bother my good friend Xiufang, who was busy taking care of her sick mother. I shared my frustrations with Ju Shi Fu and she asked me, "Why don't you talk to your mother?"

"She won't understand." I answered.

"Then, let me introduce you to a smart young man who works at the Maintenance Department next to our lab."

"I don't mean that. I want to find a friend to discuss things: books, not dating."

"You have to find a boyfriend sooner or later, and you can also discuss things with him. Do you want to get married one day?" I couldn't say no. I wanted to be a normal person like everyone else.

When I was a young woman, people courted one another mainly by being introduced through mutual friends or relatives. Love and sex were taboo subjects. They were never mentioned by our parents or relatives or written about in our textbooks. A date often consisted of a long walk in public with a supervising adult following just out of earshot. If there was an attraction between the couple, they would never kiss or exhibit any physical contact in public. They would communicate their feelings to the matchmaker who had introduced them. If both sets of parents approved of the match, then marriage would be proposed. People mainly entered marriages to carry on their family names and to have children. The whole process of courting could take from one to several years.

It turned out that Master Worker Ju was happy that Tang did not walk with me anymore because she had someone else in mind for me. The following Sunday, Ju Shi Fu came to visit my family. While I watched her two daughters playing in the attic, she talked to my mother in the kitchen.

When she left, Mama showed me a picture of the young man, whom I already knew. His name was Jianguo and he was the Youth League secretary. We held Youth League meetings once a month to read newspapers and discuss our work. He was a tall, dark and handsome guy. He seemed the exact opposite of Tang. He was very sociable and got along with people very well. That's why a lot of people liked him, including Ju Shi Fu.

On our first date, he took me to the Shanghai Cafe, a very modern and classy place for young people. I had heard about this place but I had never been there. I told him he didn't have to take me there to impress me. The coffee there was double the price of the regular coffee shops. He said he liked the atmosphere there, and he wanted to talk to me. Then he made a quite impressive speech. He said he had known me for more than three years and had never told anyone about his desire to date me until recently, when he had asked Ju Shi Fu if she was willing to carry the message and talk with me and my parents.

By any standards at that time, he was a good match for me. He was from a working family as well, had a good and stable job (he was making 42 yuan a month as a mechanic), and he said he had already saved over a thousand yuan for the future. I looked at him and wondered if I could live with him. From his serious and earnest manner, I could tell he was sincere and true.

I could probably live with him and raise a family with him just like my parents, his parents and generations before us had.

The following Sunday, he came to see my parents with the usual "Maojiao Nuxu" gifts expected on the first visit to his future in-laws. (Maojiao Nuxu literally means "hairy foot son-in-law" since the future son-in-law would be nervous and clumsy when visiting the girl's family for the first time.) According to Shanghai customs, the future son-in-law should bring the girl's father gifts of wine and cigarettes and the future mother-in-law gifts of ginseng, herbs or silk. My parents seemed pleased with his good manners and intentions, so we started dating.

Things were getting better in China and food was available as long as you had a stable job. I might have worked in the factory for the rest of my life and raised my own family until my retirement if it had not been for an unforeseen event which changed the course of my life.

In the early 1970s, the Chinese government was considering re-opening the universities and colleges and giving working class people the opportunity to obtain a higher education. As a result, the university student selection committee approached different factories, communes and army facilities to choose bright young people of good character and family backgrounds to receive this opportunity. I was one of two girls selected from my factory to attend the Shanghai Foreign Languages Institute to study English. Another two young men from our factory were also chosen to study in a technical college.

I had no idea that this selection process was going on in our factory. I only remember vaguely that I was asked to complete a form by the personnel department. One of the personnel officers asked me if I had studied English. I said that I had learned some English when I was in middle school.

When I was informed that I was going to attend the Shanghai Foreign Languages Institute to study English, I could not believe my ears. I had always dreamed of going to college and becoming a teacher someday, but I had given up that dream when I entered my work-study program a few years before. Since then I had never in my wildest dreams expected to have an opportunity like this. I had been chosen by my factory to study English at the Foreign Languages Institute. Wow!

With all the political changes going on while I was growing up, I could never predict my future. But now, out of the blue, my dreams had come true! It was really a miracle and a great surprise to me. It was also a big surprise to my parents, my whole family, and all my friends.

Jianguo was happy for me, but he was also worried that I might change my mind once I was in college. I told him that if he was worried about me changing my mind, then he did not know me well enough. I told him that I could not foretell what would happen in our future, but I had faith in us, and I also wanted to accept this new challenge.

I cherished this opportunity and was determined to succeed regardless of any obstacles. As far as I know, I was the first person in the Shen family to ever attend college. I knew it was now my obligation and duty to do my best, to face this challenge and win honor for myself, my family, and my factory. The mountain was on my back. Failure was not an option for me.

7 – College Years in Shanghai
1970-1973

In March 1970 I entered the Shanghai Foreign Languages Institute, which was later renamed the Shanghai International Studies University. It was founded in December 1949, originally known as Shanghai College of Russian. In 1963, it became a national key institution of higher learning and more languages were added, including English, French, German, Japanese, Arabic and Spanish. We were the first class to enter the institute since 1966 when the Cultural Revolution had started and the institute had been closed down.

There was a huge welcome from the whole institute for the 30 entering students. We were called the "Experimental Class" as well as the "Worker-Peasant-Soldier Students". I was one of 20 students in the English class. Seven of the students in the English class were women. Another 10 students were assigned to study German. Our English class was composed of eight workers, six peasants and six soldiers. I felt quite honored to be one of them.

The leadership committee of our Experimental Class was composed of three officials, an Army Commander, a Master Worker, and an Administrator from the institute. They oversaw the entire operation and made all decisions together. They also encouraged our professors, lecturers and all students to participate in the experiment.

On the first day, we were introduced to two older professors and two young lecturers of English who would be teaching us and living on campus with us. Professor Lu and Professor Yang were in their 60s, and Mr. He and Miss Sun were both lecturers of English in their 30s. Since our class was an experimental class, the institute provided us with the best teaching staff available from the English Department.

All the students were required to live in dormitories on the campus. We were only allowed to go home on Saturday afternoon and had to return to the campus on Sunday evening before nine o'clock. Even our professors and lecturers were required to follow this rule unless they had an emergency. At that time, everyone studied or worked six days a week. China didn't adopt the five-day-work week until 1995.

We began our intensive language studies right away, on the second day. Our daily routine was to rise at six o'clock sharp. At six-fifteen we all lined up for a 30-minute morning jog. Then we had a 15-minute break to wash up or change. From seven to seven-thirty we had breakfast in the dining hall. From seven-thirty to eight, we did our morning studies consisting of memorizing new vocabulary, spelling, and reciting texts from memory. Classes ran from eight to twelve with a 10-minute break between each class.

Our morning classes focused on English language studies. After lunch we took a short break and then resumed our classes from one to four o'clock. Afternoon classes covered other subjects such as Chinese, World History, Western Literature, Politics and International Relations. From four to five we usually had P.E. class, played ping pong or some other games for an hour. We ate dinner from five-thirty to six. After dinner, we were back in our classroom and spent at least another three hours completing our assignments or doing individual study. One teacher, sometimes two, were available to answer our questions and explain things during these study hours.

We were assigned to a dormitory with four students to a room. I shared a room with three other girls, one from a metal factory in Shanghai and the other two from People's Communes in the suburbs of Shanghai. We were all between 20 and 23 years old. In our dormitory room, there were two bunk beds on opposite walls. In the middle of the room, there was a rectangular table with four chairs where we would do our homework. Our teacher Miss Sun was assigned to the room next to ours, but she often came to our room to check on us and ask if we had any questions for her.

Guifang, my friend from our factory, was assigned to the next room. I often went to her room, and we usually did our assignments together. Guifang was the most productive and fastest weaver in our factory, and all the young girls in her department tried to catch up with her. She had held the title "Xiao Laohu" (Little Tiger) for the last few years, and everyone in our factory had called her "Xiao Laohu." I still called her "Xiao Laohu" affectionately when we were together.

Our two male professors and Mr. He were assigned to live with the students in the men's dormitory. The oldest student in our English class was 28. He was engaged to be married. Within a few months, he asked for permission to leave because he found the program to be too stressful. We were sorry to see him go, but he said with a smile, "Don't worry about me. I just can't compete with you guys, and I can't wait three more years to get married." He was the only person to drop out of our English program.

Another male student dropped out of the German class after two years in the program. He seemed to be doing fine for the first two years, but then he got sick and couldn't keep up with the rigid routine and intensive studies. He complained of continuous headaches and insomnia. The doctors advised him to take things easy and rest for a few months, but he felt he could not continue. After working so hard for two years, he had to quit the program. What a shame! We all liked him and we hoped he would recover soon.

Of the 30 matriculating students, 28 graduated from the Institute three years later. I believed those two students would have loved to complete their studies if their situations had been different. As it was, they went back to their former jobs and continued to contribute to society as they had done before.

Even though it was a tough program, I knew I could handle the pressure and the arduous studies as long as I took it one day at a time. I felt extremely fortunate to have this opportunity. There were so many young people I knew who worked as hard as I did, some even harder. Many were smarter than me, but they had not received this kind of opportunity because of family background or some other reason. I kept reminding myself: where else on earth could anyone receive such an education? Every time I thought about this my blood raced and my heart thumped faster, and I could not stop working until I was satisfied or completely exhausted.

In addition to working hard on my English and other subjects, I also participated in extra-curricular activities, such as volunteering to clean up the campus by picking up trash and sweeping the grounds and public areas. I also joined the ping pong team to compete with students from other universities. I even agreed to be a spokesperson for our student body. Whenever there were visitors from other departments or from outside the institute, I was one of three students to represent the opinions of our 20 English language students. I was chosen to represent my fellow students because at the regular meetings with the teachers, students and leadership committee, I was outspoken, not shy as most girls my age were. During one meeting, I was so involved in the discussions that I forgot my parents' warnings not to voice my opinions outside the home.

We were discussing the ways students could improve oral English rapidly. Professor Lu and Miss Sun were leading our discussion, and Mr. He was taking notes. One male student suggested that our teachers could compile an English Conversation book for us so we could read and practice every day.

"Yes, we can do that, but it takes time." Miss Sun replied.

Another male student raised his hand and jumped in, "How about watching foreign movies to improve our English and expand our vocabulary?"

"It's a good idea. But watching movies won't improve your oral English ability, only your listening ability. Furthermore, it's not easy to find the right kind of foreign movies to watch," Professor Lu commented.

Miss Sun looked at our girl students, but no one said anything. Finally, I raised my hand to contribute an idea, "We can form small groups to talk in English about our everyday life, our school, our study or anything we want to discuss. We just need a teacher in each group to listen and help us when we make mistakes or don't know how to say certain things." Everyone agreed that it was a good idea, and we decided to start our conversation groups right away.

Another time we were discussing how to squeeze our four-year curriculum into a three-year program. According to our leadership committee, we needed to spend one month each year to "learn" from workers, peasants and soldiers. At the meeting, one peasant student objected that after a whole month working with peasants in the fields, we might forget what we had already learned.

Miss Sun said, "If you bring your textbooks, we can review what we have learned and add some new vocabulary about farming, crops and local culture."

Most of the students nodded their heads, but another peasant student cautioned us, "It will be very hard to find a time and place to meet once you are working in the countryside. You will all be falling asleep after a full day's hard work."

I thought about that and turned to the Army Commander. "Commander, what's the purpose of spending one month each year to go to the factory, the countryside and the army unit?"

"The purpose is to teach all our students not to forget where they come from and to keep close ties with ordinary working-class people," the commander replied.

"What if we went there for just a week or two, to learn from them, work with them and make personal connections with them. We could also write to them, or even invite them to our campus to give us talks about their life and work. If we did that, we wouldn't forget where we come from. We could write about their stories in both Chinese and English and put them on the bulletin board. In this way, we could save some time and still retain our knowledge."

One soldier student seemed a little puzzled and asked "How about learning from soldiers?"

"We can do the same. We can still go there for a couple of weeks and come back with connections and write to soldiers regularly. It would be easier to invite drill sergeants to our campus to train us than to have 30 to 40 staff and students pack up and go to the military base for a whole month," I replied.

I knew I might be out of line, but I really cared and wanted to contribute. I sat down and waited for the responses. We were all quiet; no one said anything. Finally, the Commander said, "We had a wonderful discussion. We got some good ideas and suggestions. Thank you all for your participation. We need to discuss this issue further in our next meeting." After this meeting, I was designated as one of the three students who would represent our student body.

I cherished every moment of my college years and studied conscientiously, learning from each of our teachers and absorbing as much of their knowledge as I could.

Professor Lu, a very near-sighted English professor with a pair of extremely thick glasses, was the Department's Shakespeare expert. He said to us one day, "English is an easy language to learn at first. But the more you learn the more difficult it becomes. It is especially difficult when we use prepositions like 'in,' 'on,' or 'at' and articles like 'the.' Sometimes you don't know which one to use or whether or not we need to use 'the' because the Chinese language does not have articles and propositions. I am still confused sometimes after 40 years of speaking and teaching English."

"So, what shall we do about it?" one of the students asked.

"The general rule is that we use 'in' for places like country, city or town, etc. We use 'at' for smaller places like 'at home,' 'at college,' or 'at the swimming pool' and so on."

"But I noticed in our English textbook, we have 'in school' and 'in college," I pointed out.

"That's true, so the best advice I can give you is to pay attention to what the English and American people write and speak. Sometimes they are interchangeable. We need to follow the lead of those who live in that environment. As many people say, 'When in Rome, do as the Romans do'."

Professor Lu also had a unique sense of humor. He often provided us with vivid examples and interesting metaphors to help us learn English grammar. I still remember his special teaching style to this day. When one of us forgot to put an article in a sentence, such as: "Woman is my aunt." Professor Lu said, "You need a hat in this sentence. You need to add either 'the' or 'this' or 'that' woman is my aunt. Without a hat, it looks incomplete. It's like a bald-headed man without a hat in the winter time."

When one of our students used the wrong verb tense in a sentence, he would say, "This is a serious mistake, a disease like cancer. You must be careful when using verbs. Verbs are very important in all sentences. Just remember this: the subject is like a person's head, the verb is like the body, and the object is like your legs. You need all three parts to function properly. You can drop an article (a hat or a scarf), but you can never drop a subject (a head) or a verb (a person's body.)"

Our other English professor was Professor Yang. He was in his early 60s. In his class, we learned pronunciation, usage and structure of the English language. He was a very tall and good-looking Eurasian man. We only knew that his father was Chinese and his mother was French. Students were not supposed to ask a teacher personal questions, so we never learned the details of his background. We enjoyed Professor Yang's classes as much as Professor Lu's. He would walk around the classroom shrugging his shoulders all the time while he delivered his lectures. Suddenly he would stop beside your seat and ask you a question, so we had to pay close attention to everything he said.

Professor Yang was the main teacher who recorded all the new words and phrases for our new lessons from our textbooks. Before we learned a new lesson, we listened to Professor Yang's recordings and tried to imitate his pronunciation of each new word and new phrase as closely as we could. Then we listened to his recording while we read the text of our new lesson again and again until we had memorized it.

Miss Sun specialized in American literature. She taught us intensive and extensive reading. "Intensive reading," she said, "involves students reading in detail with specific learning aims and tasks, while extensive reading is generally to read for pleasure as well as to develop reading skills." She had a beautiful sing-song voice. Whenever she read us a short story from her literature collections, we could hear every word very clearly, and we could understand the whole story except for a few new words. I usually jotted down the phonetic sounds of the words I did not know and then checked my dictionary after the class. When we did our dictations, she read the passage twice--the first time at normal speed and the second time very slowly so that we could write down each word clearly and correctly without missing anything.

Mr. He taught us English Grammar and Translation from English to Chinese and vice-versa. He was also a brilliant lecturer and specialized in English literature. When we asked him the difference between American Literature and English Literature, he said, "American literature refers to the production of literary works of American culture and themes; while English literature refers to the collection of written literary work in Great Britain and its colonies since the seventh century to the present day. Sometimes it's confusing; but just remember that, at one time, when America was a British colony, both terms meant the same thing. It all changed when America became independent on July 4, 1776, and was no longer a British colony."

When Mr. He explained grammar to us, he explained English grammar as precisely as if he were a surgeon or a research scientist. He cut paragraphs into sentences and cut long sentences into short phrases. Then he dissected the phrases into parts of speech such as nouns, articles, verbs, adjectives, adverbs and so on. When we tried to translate English into Chinese or vice-versa, he showed us how to build sentences like building blocks and then make them into a room, a house or an apartment. His teaching style was different from other teachers. It was unique, with more imagination and precision.

Under Mr. He's guidance, we translated articles from two major newspapers--Beijing's People's Daily and Shanghai's Wen Hui Bao--from Chinese into English. We also translated articles from some foreign newspapers and magazines into Chinese. In order to have more practice, I found some passages from Charles Dicken's David Copperfield and translated them into Chinese, and then I compared my translation side by side with the published translated book I found in our library. From this kind of practice, we learned the skill of translation and gradually developed a deeper understanding and appreciation of the English language and literature.

During our first year, we spent two weeks in a commune near Shanghai, working alongside peasants in the fields. We got up very early in the morning and learned how to transplant rice seedlings in the fields. Rice seedlings should be planted at a shallow depth in straight rows. We were told to hold the stalks of the seedlings carefully to ensure their fast revival and rapid growth after transplanting. It was back-breaking and labor-intensive work. We separated the seedlings gently and then used our fingers to insert them into the muddy soil. One of the peasants we worked with taught me not to plant the seedlings too deep into the soil for fear that the stalks would not get enough oxygen to grow. After constantly bending our backs and moving our feet in the puddled field, our backs and legs started to hurt. We had to straighten up frequently and move our bare feet forward very carefully in order not to fall onto the muddy field. We had a half hour lunch break under the tree shade. Luckily, our lunches were provided by the commune and were delivered to us by the peasants who were on kitchen duty. After lunch break, we continued our work until dinner time.

We also learned how to transplant vegetable seedlings in the vegetable fields. The depth of vegetable transplanting varied depending on what kind of vegetables we were working on. Deep-rooting vegetables needed deep holes, while regular green vegetables were planted just a half inch deep. I still remember what an old peasant woman told us when we were handling seedlings, "You need to separate all the vegetable seedlings very lightly as if you are handling fresh eggs." It was a lot easier working in the vegetable field than working in the rice field. You could at least have your shoes on, and you didn't risk a fall on your butt in a muddy rice field.

We worked about 10 hours a day just like the peasants did. In the evening, we reviewed our lessons and studied long lists of vocabulary for farming tools, machines, names of crops and seeds. There were so many mosquitoes flying around us that we had to get into our mosquito nets at night to escape them. The light inside the net was very dim, so I had to squeeze my eyes hard to read. I became myopic and had to wear eyeglasses after that.

During our second year, we went to a military base to learn from soldiers. Contrary to our expectations, the military routine was much easier than working in the fields 10 hours a day. We underwent a short stint of military training. All students and teachers were assigned army buddies as soon as we arrived. We followed our buddies and did exactly what we were told. We got up as soon as we heard the horn blow at six sharp. The goal of this training was to instill in us a sense of patriotism, collectivism and national defense. Similar to our routine at the institute, we ran outside for about half an hour, had our breakfast in the dining hall, and then spent about four hours practicing drills, formations and learning how to use guns and rifles safely and accurately.

In the afternoon, we had two hours of political study and one hour of leisure activities with our army buddies. We spent time socializing and playing games with soldiers and commanders. Sometimes we helped the kitchen staff pick fresh vegetables from the fields and wash them in big basins.

I remember one afternoon we were sent with some soldiers to collect yams and potatoes. After we had dug up a lot of yams and potatoes, one of the kitchen staff said, "We have more than enough for dinner. Why don't we start a fire and roast some now. I am hungry!" We were hungry too after digging in the fields for hours. With the anticipation of eating yams and potatoes roasted over an open fire, we felt exuberant and began to sing military songs with the soldiers.

When the fire was burning red, we threw yams and potatoes into the fire, turning them periodically with long metal sticks. Not too long afterwards, the sweet, tempting smell of roasting yams and potatoes was floating in the air. We moved them to the edge of the fire and let them continue to cook in the ashes until they were blackened and charred and the skins were crisp and crunchy. Finally, we picked one up with our long sticks, peeled the skin off with paper towels, and started to eat. Some of the soldiers ate them with the burned skin still on. They were the most tasty, sweet and delicious yams and potatoes I had ever eaten in my life!

In the evenings we reviewed our lessons and studied our vocabulary of military terms and usages for another two to three hours. For our sleeping arrangements, all male students and teachers were assigned to dorms with the soldiers; while the seven female students and Miss Sun were assigned to a big storage room, since there were no female soldiers or dorms at that time.

The storage room was cold with no furniture except a big pile of hay in one corner. We used layers of hay as a mattress and spread our quilts and bedding on top. It was especially cold at night, so we all cuddled in one corner as closely as we could to keep warm and shared our quilts. Miss Sun shared her quilt with me. Once, when both my feet were icy cold, Miss Sun stretched her warmer feet out to warm my feet. I said, "You don't have to do that, Miss Sun. My feet are too cold."

Miss Sun said quietly, "Shi shi, just close your eyes and go to sleep. We have to get up early."

I was so touched. I have never forgotten her kindness and dedication to her students. I promised myself that cold winter night that I wanted to be a kind and devoted teacher just like her.

During our third year, we went to Shanghai Harbor to learn from workers. We worked eight hours a day carrying boxes and moving big or small items from one place to another. Each of us was assigned to work beside a master worker. We learned how to use our shoulders to carry boxes and how to use a big piece of cloth to move heavy items on our backs without hurting ourselves. In the evening, we again spent two to three hours reviewing our lessons, studying new vocabulary and speaking to each other in English. We had started to think in English and dream in English by then. Professor Yang said it was a good sign that we subconsciously used English all the time.

Sometimes in the harbor we would meet English-speaking sailors getting on and off their ships. We often waved to them and said "Hi." Quite often, they would stop and chat with us in English. We thought it was a good way to practice our English with foreigners. But our master workers warned us, "It's all right to practice your English with them as long as you all remember not to get on their ships when you are invited." One of the students asked why. The answer was, "Once you are on their ship, it's their territory, and they can do whatever they want to you." We appreciated their warnings and listened to their instructions closely.

All the experiences we had and the time we spent with workers, peasants and soldiers kept us deeply rooted with ordinary working people. We understood the value of this education, and we were grateful for the opportunity we received. This program was designed to teach us never to forget our roots and our responsibilities to our society and to each other. I learned how hard ordinary people just like my parents work all their lives for a living. To this day, I still remember the poem we learned when we were young: "shui zhi pen zhong can, li li jie xin ku" (each grain in your dish is packed with sweat). I have never forgotten the experiences I had working with peasants and workers and learning from soldiers. I know I am a better person because of this exposure.

We, the Experimental Class, completed a four-year curriculum in three years' time. I was 24 years old when I graduated from Shanghai Foreign Languages Institute.

In February 1973, as soon as I graduated from the English Department, I was assigned to join the faculty of that Department. My friend and co-worker from the same factory, Guifang, was assigned to work in the library of our English Department; later she was transferred to the main library of the university. She worked there until her retirement. Jade, the peasant student sharing the same dorm with me was also assigned to work at the institute, but later she was given a new challenge--to study Albanian in Tirana. As the friendship between China and Albania had developed, it had become important to have another language, Albanian, available at our institute.

I remember during one summer, Guifang and I went to visit Jade in Nanxiang People's Commune where she lived. We rode our bikes for an hour and a half from our campus to Nanxiang Ancient Town where we stopped to eat this town's famous soup dumplings. Nanxiang, located in the northwest of Jiading district of Shanghai, has a history going back 1500 years and is one of the four most famous historical and cultural towns in Shanghai.

After a bowl of delicious noodle soup and some dumplings, we continued our bike ride for another 20 minutes before we arrived at Jade's home. Jade's mother was a typical peasant woman with a great smile and generous heart. She insisted on feeding us her homemade sweet egg soup and fresh vegetables from her garden. Jade's father worked in a factory in the northern part of China. She had only one brother and one sister. After lunch, we visited their backyard garden where they grew sugarcane and vegetables. Jade started to cut down sugar cane with her siblings and showed us how to eat it on the spot. We chewed and sucked the juice out of the sugarcane; it was the best sugarcane we had ever tasted. Jade's mother gave us a bunch to take home.

A couple of weeks later, Jade came to visit me and my family, and we planned to visit Guifang the following day. After we had a simple dinner of rice and steamed fish, my siblings were still sitting around the table discussing things as usual. Even our two youngest siblings joined the conversation. I listened to them while washing the dishes nearby, as it was my turn to do the dishes that night. Everyone had his or her opinions and ideas. Jade was very surprised and asked, "Do you always have lively conversations like this?"

"Sure we do, almost every day. Our parents encourage us to say anything we want at home. They just want us to be careful outside home," I replied.

"No wonder you always have good ideas and always have something to say at our meetings. In my family we are always quiet. We don't talk when we eat," Jade said.

"Maybe you don't have as many siblings as I do." I wiped my hands and Jade helped me put the clean dishes away. My two young sisters continued their conversation all the way up to the attic to go to sleep. They were still talking in the dark after the lights were out.

Finally our mother said, "Jade must be tired coming all the way here. It's time to sleep. Even though it's summer vacation, you still have to get up early in the morning."

All these years, I have had so many wonderful memories of our times together in school, in my friends' homes and in my home. It was amazing that I always had good luck in meeting a few good friends here and there along the way.

Just before my graduation, I shared the good news about my graduation with Ju Shi Fu and other former co-workers at the factory who had supported me and cheered me on during the past three years. Ju Shi Fu was so happy and proud of me that she gave me a gold-plated ink pen as a graduation gift. I treasured it and used it for a long time during my teaching career.

Jianguo was also excited for me although we had not seen each other often during the last three years. I saw him about once a month at either my parents' home or his parents' home. We never went out for fun or any kind of entertainment.

After graduation, my first assignment was to assist Mrs. Margaret Wang, an English language expert from Scotland. She had married a Chinese man who was also an English teacher in a local middle school. Mrs. Wang had lived and worked in China for over 20 years before I met her. The Chinese government gave special considerations to foreigners like Mrs. Wang who had lived in China and had served China for a long time. Her family lived in a big apartment with three to four bedrooms assigned by the institute. Her apartment was much bigger than a regular teacher's apartment. I was assigned a one-bedroom apartment when I got married three years later.

My responsibility was to assist Mrs. Wang for her class preparations and any other things relating to her work since she could not speak Chinese. The lecturer who had assisted her was on maternity leave. Some people told me that Mrs. Wang was a very fussy lady, and it was difficult to work with her. But after working with her for a while, I found that she was in fact an excellent teacher who was simply strict and outspoken. She often became frustrated when some of the supporting staff in the English Department did not understand her requests in English. We became quite close after working together for a few months, and she invited me to her apartment several times to have afternoon tea with her.

Besides assisting Mrs. Wang, I also taught first year English and pronunciation. Most of our new students were workers, peasants and soldiers from other cities and provinces of China. They had a hard time pronouncing "l," "n," "r," and some other English consonants, which had no similar sound in their local dialects. I learned how to be patient with them and practiced with them over and over again until they got the pronunciation right.

I also learned quite a few English and Scottish slang words from Mrs. Wang because she was a native English speaker. When I met Mrs. Wang for meetings in her office or at her home, she would often ask me, "Would you like a cuppa?" "Cuppa" meant a cup of tea. Other Scottish phrases she used included "Let me have a swatch (a quick look)." and "Just give me a wee bit (a small amount)."

Sometimes when we had a few minutes to spare, she asked to learn a few Chinese phrases from me, such as "Zai Jian!" (See you later), "Hao jile!" (Good job) and "Tai Meile" (Very beautiful). Mrs. Wang was indeed a dedicated and hard-working teacher, and we got along very well.

A few months after I had started assisting Mrs. Wang, the Dean of the English Department informed me that I had been selected by our institute for further studies abroad. There were only three candidates selected from Shanghai by the Educational Bureau of Higher Learning to travel to England to study English for two years. The other two were young men, one from Fudan University and the other from the Shanghai Foreign Languages High School attached to the Foreign Languages Institute where I was teaching.

When I heard this, I was speechless. I didn't know what to say. I was happy with my assignment and teaching duties; since I was learning to be the best teacher I could be, like all my mentors before me. But going to England to study for two more years? That was incredible! I couldn't wait to tell my parents the wonderful news! I was so excited that night that I couldn't fall asleep. I thought I might as well get up and start preparing for the English examinations in Beijing. Only those who passed those exams would be sent on to the British Consulate for an interview.

I had two weeks to prepare a young teacher Yongxin to take over my work and my responsibilities in the English Department. Yongxin was a fast learner and was very polite, but a little nervous in front of Mrs. Wang. I told him to relax and be himself. Mrs. Wang was not as fussy as other people had said. After about a week he was comfortable, so I said good-bye to all my co-workers and friends and went home to prepare myself for the upcoming tests in Beijing.

After a couple of more weeks' preparation, I took the express train to Beijing. I was to stay at Beijing Language Institute for testing and orientation. I met all the candidates from 10 major universities across China. We sat for both written and oral examinations. Those who passed the exams went to the British Consulate for an interview, and those who had not passed the examinations returned to their work units for future opportunities. Roughly 80 percent of the candidates passed the tests. I was one of them.

After the interview at the British Consulate, we had a two-week orientation at the Beijing Language Institute. I was lucky enough to be in a group of 12 selected to go to England at that time. I was one of only two women chosen.

I had never, ever dreamed of going abroad! Not to mention going to England to study! What an extraordinary opportunity I had been given! Once again, the mountain was on my back, but I was eager for the adventure that lay ahead.

8 – Further Studies in England
1973-1975

I arrived at Heathrow Airport in London on October 27, 1973, just a few days before my 25th birthday. For the first time in my life I was far away from home in a foreign land that I had only read about. This was also the first time out of the country for the only other female traveler in our group. Her name was Helena and she was in her early 30s. Her eyes were still wet from saying good-bye to her family. After the plane took off, she told me that her son was only three years old and she had already started missing her little boy. "Who is taking care of him while you are away?" I asked.

"My husband and his parents," she replied.

"That must be tough for all of you."

"Yes, but I can't pass up this opportunity to study in England, you know."

I learned from our conversation that she had been an interpreter for the Central Propaganda Department for the last few years. I understood that she had to make sacrifices for her career. I was glad I did not have to make this kind of tough decision. Little did I know; my turn would come later in my life.

When we were waiting for our luggage, I was filled with excitement, anticipation and anxiety towards this unknown land. A special coach from the Embassy took us to No. 10 Eaton

Avenue in London. This was a special hostel run by the Chinese Embassy to temporarily house visiting scholars and students upon their arrival in England and during their holidays when schools were closed. Mr. Lei, a diplomat from our Embassy, welcomed us and took us to the dining room where a delicious meal of noodles awaited us.

I had been airsick on the plane and had eaten very little during the last leg of our journey. Now, seeing everyone hungrily gulping down the food, my appetite returned. I ate two full bowls of noodles with lots of vegetables and some stir-fry chicken dishes. After that, we all retired to our rooms and wrote letters to our families in China. I slept through Friday and Saturday, recovering from the jet-lag.

On Sunday someone suggested we visit Hyde Park. I had only read about the Speakers' Corner in Hyde Park and was excited to join the group. When we got to the park, we saw a few people standing on soap boxes, speaking loudly and surrounded by crowds of listeners. Most of the listeners appeared to be tourists and foreigners like us. We joined the crowd and listened to several speakers. These included an old man wearing a suit of shabby clothes with funny marks on his face and a young black man in blue jeans and a yellow jacket speaking at the top of his lungs to make people laugh. He was like a comedian. I could not figure out what they were talking about and why some people were laughing. The only English words I could understand were "Money, money".

I was surprised to see there were no police around, and people seemed relaxed and colorful. Strolling in the park with my friends, I noticed that there were a lot of old ladies, with colorful clothes and pretty make-up on their faces, sitting alone here and there on the benches in the sunshine. Some young couples walked hand-in-hand with their children running behind them. I wondered why there were so many old people sitting alone without their families. I also wondered why these young couples were holding each other's hands instead of holding their children's hands. This surprised me, as it would be just the opposite in China. The young couples would have been holding their children's hands, and the old people would have been with their families instead of sitting alone in the park. It was my first dose of culture shock.

We spent our first week at the British Council, which provided us with brief introductory lectures on Britain. We enjoyed tours to different places in London. We visited the Tower of London, Westminster Abbey, the Houses of Parliament, St. Paul's Cathedral and a local elementary school on the outskirts of London. The lectures and visits arranged by the British Council gave us an excellent introduction to British history and culture.

One of the tour guides was a pretty young woman with a huge dog following her all the time. We asked her the dog's name and how old the dog was. She replied proudly, "His name is Sam and he's almost five years old." Sam waggled his tail and licked her hands and face before lying down next to her seat on the bus. She said proudly, patting Sam's head, "He is such a sweet boy. He is better than my two ex-husbands." This was my second cultural shock during my first week in London. Why did she call her dog a sweet boy? How could a dog be better than two men? This young woman had divorced twice, but in China we seldom heard of a divorced man or woman.

After about a week touring London and seeing places of interest, we were eager and ready to begin our study. I was assigned to a group of 10 students to be trained as teachers. Helena, the interpreter I met on the plane, went with another group to be trained as journalists and interpreters at another school. On the morning of November 4, we left London for Folkstone, a seaside resort not far from London. Mr. Peter O'Connell, the principal of the Folkstone School of English Studies, welcomed us at the Commons Room with a group of teaching staff.

Mr. O'Connell was an aristocratic-looking, middle-aged English gentleman. As soon as we sat down, he began his welcome speech. "Ladies and gentlemen, allow me on behalf of all our teaching staff and students here to welcome the second group of Chinese students to our school. The students in the last group have left a deep impression on us. From you Chinese young people, we have learned how industrious and hard-working the great Chinese people are. I hope you will enjoy studying here. All the teachers and staff will be happy to assist you in any way we can." I still have a photograph of Mr. O'Connell with our group of 10 students and his teaching staff taken on our first day at the Folkstone School of English Studies.

Then he introduced us to Mrs. Harrison who was in charge of our accommodations. She divided us into pairs and assigned us to five families. Miss Kuo and I were assigned to Mr. and Mrs. Brown. Miss Kuo was from a rural peasant family near Beijing and was also a "worker-peasant-soldier" student at Beijing University. She had been working as a teaching assistant at Beijing University, just like me.

After a short chat with our host families, the other four pairs of Chinese students were driven to their new homes. Miss Kuo and I had to wait because our landlord, Mr. Brown, was still working and his wife did not have the family car. Our principal, Mr. O'Connell volunteered to drive us to the Browns and helped us carry our heavy trunks upstairs. Mrs. Brown, a plump young woman in her 30s, showed us our bedroom consisting of two twin beds and one chair. She said, "There is no room to put a desk here for you, but you can use our dining table downstairs to do your homework."

We expressed our thanks and followed her downstairs. We played with the Browns' two little girls who were three and five years old while Mrs. Brown prepared the family dinner. These girls were very cute and were murmuring to themselves. Around six o'clock, Mr. Brown and their two teenage daughters, aged 13 and 15, arrived home. This meal was our first introduction to an English family dinner. We were served baked chicken, potatoes and brussels sprouts. I had never eaten brussels sprouts in China, so I asked Mrs. Brown, "What do you call these little cabbages?" She told me what they were called, and I thought to myself as I ate them, "These brussels sprouts have no flavor, but they are rather tender and are quite different from regular cabbages."

After supper we talked with the Browns but were often interrupted by their children's screaming. We learned that Mr. Brown worked in a local post office and his wife took care of their four children. She took in foreign students to supplement the family budget. They were not very talkative; and we were tired, so we thanked them for the nice meal, said good night and went upstairs to our room.

Our bedroom was cold, and there was scarcely any space to move about. Miss Kuo and I had to share a small closet, so we left most of our clothes in our trunks leaned against the wall. Linda, their second daughter, knocked and then opened our door asking if we would like to have a fire. We said, "Yes, please." Then her father lit a kerosene stove, and she brought it into our room saying, "Mummy said you should turn it off before going to sleep."

We unpacked some of our stuff and sat on our narrow beds discussing how we should establish good relations with the Browns. After a while we washed up in the small bathroom that we would share with the two teenage girls. Then we turned off the stove to sleep. It did not give much warmth but emanated quite noxious fumes from the kerosene. That was our first night in Folkstone with an English family. I went to bed feeling cold and a little homesick.

Everything went smoothly at school the next day. All the teaching staff and students were very friendly. We had started our courses in the middle of the term, so we attended a special tutoring class to catch up. Mr. Scott, who had just arrived in Folkstone from Scotland, was our tutor. He was only 28 years old, but looked much older because he had a beard and long hair. Another teacher from the Listening Center, Mrs. Alison, was particularly kind and helpful to us. She offered to teach us songs every Friday afternoon after class. The first song she taught us was Scotland the Brave. She was a Scot and was very proud of her heritage.

After a week in our landlady's home, we found that it was impossible to do our homework in the evenings. We tried to do our homework on the dining table in the kitchen, but the TV was too loud, and the two small children were running around screaming all the time. Consequently, our homework in the first week was done kneeling beside our beds, spreading books and dictionaries on the bed or on the floor and writing on top of the hard covers of our file folders.

One morning, Mr. O'Connell came into our classroom and asked, "Are you settling down all right? Are you happy with your families? If you have any problems, don't swallow them, just let me or Mrs. Harrison know." Miss Kuo and I decided to have a talk with Mrs. Harrison the next day. When we told Mrs. Harrison that our room was too small and we had no place to do our homework, she was very angry with the Browns.

"I told them beforehand that all Chinese students study very hard and they need to provide the desks and chairs for you. I will warn her and find you another family," she apologized.

"We have no complaints about Mrs. Brown. They treat us well. The only problem is that the study conditions are not good." We asked Mrs. Harrison not to say anything negative to our landlady.

The following noon we went home for lunch as usual. No sooner had I swallowed the first mouthful of food than Mrs. Brown burst out, "What did you say to Mrs. Harrison? I cannot help it if my children are noisy."

Kuo and I put down our forks. I said, "We told Mrs. Harrison that you treat us well. We only complained about the study conditions. We have no place to do our homework."

"But I let you use the table in the kitchen," Mrs. Brown said.

"Yes, you did. But you need the kitchen table, too. You need to prepare the food and the children are running around," Miss Kuo replied.

"Well then, pack your suitcase and go to a hotel tonight!" We were shocked at this angry and rude statement. We left the kitchen and went back to school without eating lunch. We were the first arrivals in class that afternoon. During tea break, we received a note from Mrs. Harrison with the name of our new landlady and the new address. The note stated that we were to arrive on the following Sunday morning at 10 o'clock. We thanked Mrs. Harrison and looked forward to moving to our new family.

When we returned home that evening, both Mr. and Mrs. Brown were home. Mr. Brown spoke quite a lot for a change. He said that it was their first time to have Chinese students. They had a German student, two French girls, and an African student before us, but they never studied at home and always came home very late in the evenings.

"And they often gave us presents and sometimes money," interrupted Linda, their second daughter, who sat on the floor watching TV.

"Shut up!" the father demanded.

"Well, Mr. and Mrs. Brown, we don't have time to play like other foreign students," Miss Kuo said.

Mrs. Brown joined us and said, "You won't say to Mrs. Harrison that I treated you badly?"

I said, "No, in fact we told her both of you treated us well, and we like your cooking too." She seemed reassured with this response and we were relieved as well. We waited patiently for the coming Sunday.

Trouble never comes singly. That Sunday proved to be a cold, wet and miserable day. About half past nine, two of the male students from our group came to help us carry our luggage; none of the Chinese students had a car. Following Mrs. Harrison's directions, we walked for about 20 minutes before we found the address and arrived at our new home at exactly 10:00 a.m. We rang the doorbell several times, but no one answered the door. Our school was just three blocks away, so someone suggested we go to the principal's home next to the school building for help.

Our friends went home, and we went to see the principal. Fortunately, Mr. O'Connell was at home. We briefly explained our problem. He told us maybe our new landlady had gone to church. He offered to let us sit down and watch TV in his home while we waited. Although it was cold outside, we had warm clothes on and decided to go back and wait on the porch of our new residence. He told us to return if we still had trouble.

We often heard the phrase "An Englishman's home is his castle", so we took it literally. We felt that we should not intrude upon the principal and his family on Sunday. We had nowhere to go and no lunch to eat because all the shops were closed on Sundays. We stopped by our new place and rang the bell again. Still, there was no one home. We had to find some way to kill time. We walked to a nearby shopping center looking for a place to eat and get warm. The whole place was closed down. We tried several small side streets without success either. We were getting hungrier and colder and needed to find something to eat.

While passing the King's Garden public park, we spotted a small bookstore that was open. It mainly sold newspapers, postcards and magazines, but we found some chocolate bars on one of the shelves. It was not what we really wanted, but it was better than nothing. We bought two packages of chocolate bars and devoured them right away.

In the afternoon it started drizzling, and we were getting wet. We found shelter under a big tree. Standing under the big tree and watching the rain, I was feeling quite forlorn and homesick. Our hands and feet were numb from the cold. At about five o'clock, after seven hours of waiting, we left the park and plodded towards our new residence.

Our two trunks on the staircase were gone. We rang the bell. A tall, elderly woman answered the door. She apologized for being absent and invited us into her home. She told us that she had misread the note and thought we were coming on Monday. We put our wet overcoats in the hallway, and she led the way to our bedroom. It was a big room with two full-size beds and two desks with chairs. As long as we could do our homework, we were happy.

Our second landlady, Mrs. Clemow, was a widow in her early 60s. She seemed very formal and businesslike at first, but the more we got to know her the better we liked her. She asked us what kind of food we liked and made special efforts to get the ingredients for us. Sometimes she would let us cook Chinses dishes during the weekend. We made dumplings in her kitchen for our school party, and she even joined us and helped us make the dumplings. We practiced English with her, and she showed us her family photos when her husband was still alive and working in Algeria in the 1960s.

She had two married daughters, and her 85-year-old mother was living not too far away from her home. We never met her daughters, but her mother visited her sometimes. One cold and windy Saturday morning, we returned home from the town library and saw Mrs. Clemow's mother standing outside the door trembling with cold. She did not have the key to her daughter's home. I quickly opened the door for her and helped her into the living room. Miss Kuo offered her a cup of hot tea. While sipping her tea, she coughed and said, "God bless you girls, you are so kind." Then she continued, "I waited for more than an hour. If I go home, it will cost me another 30 cents without seeing my daughter."

About one hour later, our landlady returned and said to her mother, "I told you on the phone last night that you shouldn't come out in such bad weather."

"I am in dread of loneliness, and I just want company." She was nearly crying, "Oh dear, I am too old, no one cares about me. I'd rather die..."

"For goodness sake, stop it!" our landlady snapped and left the room to prepare lunch.

We left the living room and returned to our bedroom. I sat on my bed wondering what on earth had caused the relationship between a mother and a daughter to deteriorate like this. A day in our landlady's life consisted of getting up early in the morning to cook our breakfasts, dashing to a store at nine where she worked as a part-time cashier, preparing lunch for us at noon, and then getting dinner ready for us at six. She lived a busy and lonely life. I wondered why our landlady and her mother could not live together and help each other. Life would be much easier and cheaper for them. How could family members treat one another so coldly? There was no connection and no love between them. We felt sorry for both of them.

At school we met students from different countries of the world. One special friend we made was an Argentine medical doctor, Simon. He was in his mid-60s and was also studying English. From his broken English, we learned that he had gone to China a few years before his retirement and had spent more than six months visiting Beijing, Shanghai, and Nanjing. He had been treated so well everywhere he went in China that he wanted to make friends with us. He had a very nice car and offered to take us on a day trip to the English countryside.

We gladly accepted his kind invitation. Although we left on a cold, overcast Sunday morning in February, we still saw some beautiful scenery along the way. The English countryside was so green that we felt like we were wrapped in a huge green blanket under the grayish-blue sky. We could also see a myriad of multi-colored wild flowers spread across the varying hues of green that tinted the fields and hills as far as our eyes could see. It was magnificent.

Simon drove us to Dover and then to Canterbury to visit Canterbury Cathedral. I did not know until then that this Cathedral had played an important role in England's religious history nor that the Archbishop of the Cathedral still lived there. We were all enchanted by the Cathedral's architecture and ancient feel.

It was well past one o'clock before we ate our lunch. Simon had prepared some boiled eggs, fruit and tea for us. He was like an uncle to us, driving us around and taking care of everything. After lunch Simon took us to Wye College, which was part of the University of London. We visited two young Mexican friends of his who were studying chemistry at the college. They greeted us warmly and showed us their campus and the college greenhouse. Then we all had a long conversation in their commons room. These students expressed their wishes to visit China, and we also hoped to meet again in China. We exchanged our names and phone numbers. Simon was a great friend. We continued our friendship with him even after we left Folkstone.

As Easter approached, so did the end of our courses at Folkstone. We held a farewell party at school and invited our teachers, host families and all our friends. Each of us prepared a special dish, and the school provided drinks and the conference room. Everyone enjoyed the food and the conversations with each other very much. The principal expressed his thanks and handed each of us a photo taken of the group when we first arrived in Folkstone. We also expressed our thanks to the principal, the teachers, the host families and all our friends for their support and friendship.

I never really felt at home with our host families in England, but I felt at home in our London student hostel. There we spent our Easter vacation with almost 80 other Chinese students from different language schools and universities from all over Great Britain. At last we could have our long-awaited and much longed-for Chinese food again. We also were able to speak Chinese again. Miss Kuo found her friends from Beijing University, and I found mine from Shanghai. We chit-chatted for a long time. It was also fun to visit parts of London we had not visited before. The Easter holiday passed too quickly for us, but it had alleviated some of our homesickness.

On April 7, 1974, we left London for our next destination, Eastbourne. Everything seemed brighter and busier there in comparison to Folkstone. I suppose this may have been due to the change in seasons and our elevated mood after the Easter holidays. Looking through the bus windows, we could see green hills, trees and lawns with quite a variety of hues and shades of green. I really loved the unique English landscape and all the shades of green.

About three hours later, our bus arrived at Mead's School of English. Jane, the daughter of the principal, was waiting for us. She was in charge of our housing arrangements. She greeted us warmly and transferred us to several taxis. She was so efficient that in about half an hour we were all settled in with our new host families.

My third family was the Taylors. Mr. Taylor worked in a factory as an electrician and his wife worked part-time in a small flower shop. "Now," Mrs. Taylor stated forthrightly upon our arrival, "I don't need to work there anymore. I can make money from you." That seemed to be her primary motivation for having us at her home.

When she showed us around the house, I noticed that it was large and roomy in comparison to the two English homes in which I had previously lived. Mrs. Taylor seemed polite and talkative in the beginning. I was happy that we could practice our English with her. On our first day Mr. Taylor drove us around the town and took us to the beach. The white chalk cliffs were so steep that I felt dizzy when I stood on the edge and looked down into the sea. He told us this was a place where many people chose to plunge to their deaths in the sea. Pointing to his right, Mr. Taylor said, "Can you see the lighthouse over there on the small island?"

"Yes, it seems so very tiny," I answered.

"I once repaired the electric equipment there."

"How did you get there?" Miss Kuo asked.

"I went there in a small boat."

I could not help thinking that the isolation of the lighthouse was just like the isolation of the British Isles surrounded by water. It reminded me of my separation from my family and friends in China.

Mrs. Taylor drove us to school for the first few days but then commented that petrol was very expensive so she would not be driving us to school any more. She told us to either walk to school or take the bus. We thanked her for taking us to school and started walking to school the next day.

It was about a 45-minute walk from our house to school, but the route zigzagged through a tangle of side streets and many junctions. I have never been good at navigating in new places. Spreading out our maps and looking carefully every time we turned, we still lost our way several times. One time, walking back from school, we walked the wrong way on King's Drive for more than twenty minutes. We wanted to ask directions, but not a single soul could be seen wherever we looked. We had to retrace our steps and eventually came across an old man walking his dog. He gave us directions, and after almost two hours, we finally found a familiar street. We got home a little after six, a bit late for dinner.

Mrs. Taylor was angry with us for being late. We apologized and said nothing more. I simply did not know the reason why we often lost our way in Britain. But to us all the houses and roads looked the same. It took us nearly a week to get to know the town and the route to school from our new home.

As I got to know Mrs. Taylor, I found her to be a mean person. One weekend our tutor arranged a trip to Brighton which is also known as "London on the water". We went to see a Dolphin performance and tour the city. The teacher told us to bring our lunch with us. Mrs. Taylor wrapped us a few biscuits and two small, wrinkled apples that looked like an old woman's gnarled fists. When we opened our lunch, our friends laughed and offered to share their ham and turkey sandwiches with us. We could not understand her mindless stinginess.

During our weekends, the Taylor's did not like us to stay home and study. "Why don't you go out and enjoy yourselves?" Mrs. Taylor would say. "You are so young; it's a shame to stay indoors and study all the time."

"We need to catch up with our readings and do homework during the weekends," I explained.

"All work and no play makes Jack a dull boy," Mr. Taylor said sarcastically.

We did not say anything but continued our studies as usual.

One Saturday, Mr. and Mrs. Taylor set off to the beach to enjoy the sunshine and left us a tin of soup and some bread on the table for lunch. In the evening, we were watching a TV program which our teacher had assigned to us. Half-way through the program, the old couple returned home and Mr. Taylor went straight to the TV. Without uttering a word, he changed the channel to a soccer match. Mrs. Taylor asked, "Are you girls watching the serial?"

"Yes, our teacher told us to follow the program," we responded. She glanced at her husband, who sat like a stone statue frowning and ignoring us. After a while, we tiptoed out of the TV room and returned to our bedroom.

Next morning, our landlady told us, "My husband is a bit cross with you. You left us so suddenly last night." We said we were not interested in the soccer game, and we did not want to waste our time.

The following Friday we met some friends after school, and they offered to take us to London for the weekend. We were excited and phoned our landlady right away. It would be good for all of us. We expected her to be happy that they could save food and money while we were away since that was exactly what she had encouraged us to do.

We returned from a happy and much too short weekend in time for Sunday dinner. As soon as we entered the house, we went to the living room where they were both watching TV. We greeted them, but they neither answered us nor turned their heads. We sat down on the empty sofa and waited. Without looking at us, Mrs. Taylor said,

"You girls had a good time, I suppose?"

"Yes, we did. We met a lot of friends at the embassy," we replied cheerfully, trying to be polite.

"Why didn't you tell us earlier? You spoiled our food, you know!" Mr. Taylor burst out.

I tried to control my temper, "We phoned you about four o'clock, as soon as we knew."

"But I did all the shopping for the whole week," Mrs. Taylor said, her eyes still fixed on the TV.

"How could we foretell that our friends would offer to take us to London?" Miss Kuo said and continued, "You treat us as if we are small children," Miss Kuo tried hard to control her tears. "We try very hard to cooperate with you, but you are never satisfied."

All our good intentions, naïve expectations and cooperation were pricked like soap bubbles. We left the room. We were both sad and emotionally exhausted. Lying down on my bed, I thought long and hard about this situation. There was no prospect of improving our relationship or changing their attitudes toward us and our study habits. The only way out was to find another family again. So we told Jane we needed to move and why. We moved the following Sunday.

Mr. Taylor was working overtime when we left, so Mrs. Taylor saw us off. "I am sorry you want to leave," she said. "I'm happy with you, only my husband is a bit stubborn. Now, I have to work in the flower shop again." Then she kissed us good-bye. We were very happy to be out of that negative environment.

Our fourth host family was Mr. and Mrs. Butteriss who were both in their mid-50s. Mrs. Butteriss's elderly mother also lived with them. They were the best of our four host families and we grew to love and respect them greatly.

The Butterisses were a modest, congenial and sensible couple. They had no car, no color TV, no fancy furniture, but I could feel the warm atmosphere as soon as I entered their home. It immediately reminded me of my parents, my grandmother and my family in China. Mr. Butteriss worked for a computer company. He took the train to work early in the morning and came home punctually for dinner each day. Mrs. Butteriss did all the housework and looked after her aging mother. Being Chinese, we appreciated this arrangement very much, for this is the way families function in China. We both finally felt at home.

What we liked most was that we had the same tastes in selecting TV programs. We all loved to watch the news, classic movies and ballet together. They often discussed the programs with us afterwards. This was of immense help in improving our English and understanding of British society. Whenever Mr. Butteriss came across some interesting newspaper articles, he would save them and bring them home to discuss with us in the evenings.

One evening after tea, we sat around the table in the garden and talked about the economic crisis occurring in England. Mrs. Butteriss was worried about their daughter's wedding expenses. Their daughter and future son-in-law wanted to buy a house near Birmingham where they both worked. But they could not afford to buy a house.

"I have been through two wars. I saw with my own eyes the boom, crisis and depression in this country. This time is the worst of all. I often wonder what will happen to my children and their children. I really don't know. There's no light on the horizon," Mr. Butteriss shook his head sadly.

Our hearts were heavy, but my mind was busy thinking about what he had said. How true it was that there was no light on the horizon. Silence prevailed in the garden, then Mrs. Butteriss rose from her chair, "It's getting dark. Let's go inside the house."

Mr. Butteriss stretched out his arm, pointing at the sign across the street, "Can you see the fish and chip shop over there?" We nodded. "It used to close at midnight. But now it closes at eight o'clock, sometimes at nine, because very few people can afford to go out to eat."

Mr. and Mrs. Butteriss were the kindest couple we met in England. No wonder her mother said to us when we went to say good night to her, "I am very lucky to have such a good daughter and son-in-law. Did you read the paper? One old lady in our neighborhood just died. No family was around, and no one even knew until the police broke in."

When I recall those days, I am very grateful to this family and their kindness to us. I learned firsthand how English people lived during that period. People are different from place to place, but the kindness and love this family had shown toward one another were the same as I had known in China, no matter what language they spoke or what culture they were from. I felt at home because it reminded me of my family, my parents, my grandma and great aunt.

The Meads School of English was a very small private school located in the center of town. They had only four English language classes for foreign students taught by a handful of teaching staff. We rarely saw the principal, but his son and his son-in-law both taught classes. I was in the advanced class taught by Mr. Smith, who was considered the best teacher at the school. Although only in his early 40s, he had had several interesting careers. He had been a soldier, a journalist, an interpreter of Arabic language and a teacher.

He worked very hard to support his three daughters who were in a private school in Eastbourne where their mother was the headmistress. He shared with us his ambition to establish his own language school. Once he told the class, "When my daughters grow up, I want them to elope with millionaires so that I needn't spend any money." I thought he was joking.

Reflecting on the depression in England at that time, I felt I had perhaps judged our former landladies too harshly for being mean and stingy. These happened to be the hardest economic times in England since World War II. People's living standards had been drastically reduced by inflation, unemployment and "redundancy" (job layoffs). The ordinary working people were hit the hardest and most seriously victimized by this economic crisis.

In his ministerial broadcast, the then Prime Minister, Mr. Heath said, "In this grave emergency facing the country... we are asking you to cut down to the absolute minimum the use of electricity for heating and all other purposes in your homes. We are limiting the use of electricity by almost all factories, shops and offices to three days a week." I was surprised to hear that but was thankful that they didn't cut schools to three days a week. I grew to feel more and more sympathetic towards the regular British people.

In the middle of June, our courses in Eastbourne came to an end. We were reluctant to say good-bye to the Butterisses. Thanks to the help of our teachers and families, we were making excellent progress with our English language studies. As one of our teachers put it, "You have grown from teenagers to adults. Your English writing skills have improved to college level."

On June 30, after a two-week holiday in London, we caught a train to Norwich Station and then took taxicabs to our new residential hall at the University of East Anglia in Norwich for our summer program. In this language school, we had a different kind of arrangement that suited us perfectly. We lived in the student residence hall on the university campus and studied at the Bell School of Language.

This was one of three Bell Language Schools in England. Mr. Ian Bell was the principal of the Norwich school. The other two schools, located in Cambridge and Bath, were administered by the head principal of the Bell Language Schools. His name was also Bell, so people referred to him as "Old Bell". It was a coincidence that the names of the schools and the two principals were all "Bell."

Our principal, Mr. Ian Bell, was a Catholic and an Irishman in his late 30s. He had 10 children, was tall and athletic and had a wonderful sense of humor. He arranged our course into two parts. Two months were spent in Norwich doing language studies and one month in Birmingham doing community project work. The Bell School also arranged frequent trips to different places for us to meet local people.

Our English teacher was Mrs. Benze, a very gentle, sweet young woman in her early 30s, with big, clear brown eyes and freckles on her face. She was patient with us and always smiled, even when we made mistakes. She reminded me of my elementary school teacher, Mrs. Zheng. I found it more comfortable and efficient to learn the language in a relaxed environment. Mrs. Benze became another role model for me. I aspired to provide the same kind of supportive learning environment for my students when I returned to teach in China that she provided for us in England.

The second part of our course was to choose a community project and write a report. Since Birmingham was one of the important industrial cities in Britain, I chose the manufacturing industry as my project. Other project topics included politics, education, media, religion and recreation. Our project tutor was David, a local man who knew the Birmingham area very well. He was in his late 20s and had been a milkman before becoming a tutor. He arranged some lectures and visits for our group from which we learned a great deal about the city of Birmingham.

One of our visits was to a factory that produced a wide range of water, gas and oil taps (calves) sold in Britain as well as abroad. When we were in the factory reception room, two well-dressed gentlemen handed us some fancy, colorful brochures displaying their products. In contrast, when we went into the workshop, I noticed most of the machines were semi-automatic and some were very old. Workers were busy operating the machines manually with a rhythmic pedaling of their feet. Working conditions were noisy and suffocating inside the workshop with poor air circulation, low ceilings and dim lighting. I was very surprised to find poorer working conditions in this plant than those I had experienced in Shanghai.

There was a foundry where iron and steel were melted, then molded or pressed by machines into taps. The melting iron emitted clouds of fetid, strong-smelling fumes and smoke. The last workshop we visited was where the finishing work was done. Most of workers were elderly female immigrants from India and Pakistan. There were no protective devices around the machines, and the workers were not wearing protective goggles or caps to protect their eyes or hair. The flying metal waste, droplets of oil, and dirt scattered onto their clothes, hair and faces. The whole workshop was filthy and polluted with heavy, acrid fumes. After about twenty minutes in the confines of the place, we could hardly breathe and had to hurry outside for fresh air. I felt sorry for those women who had to stay inside all day.

On another occasion, our tutor took us to see a depressed area in Birmingham where one of David's friends worked as a social worker. He parked the car in a shabby, dirty lane where a group of curious children with filthy clothes, runny noses and untidy hair rushed up and surrounded us. David's friend, a thin young woman, came out to greet us. She took us into a daycare center for the children of poor working people staffed by volunteers like her. This ramshackle building had been a warehouse and was dark, dirty and in general disrepair. Gray sky peeked through the broken roof in many places; we had to step around piles of rubbish and puddles of water on the floor.

Used clothes hung in one corner, and an old woman was putting more clothes on the racks. "This is for a jumble sale," she said. "We collect clothes for sale and get money to pay for the bus fares for the children to go to parks. These children's parents must work, and the children have no room to play in their tiny apartments. It's dangerous to let them wander about and play in the streets, so we organized this children's club to arrange safe activities for them during the day." We were touched by the volunteers who tried their best to take care of the children.

Such experiences significantly increased my understanding of Britain.

The three months we spent at Bell School passed rapidly. Our embassy had arranged for us, the future teachers of the English language, to spend our last year in the Coventry College of Education in the City of Coventry, Warwickshire. We spent a few days resting and relaxing at our London hostel. Once again, we began the tedious business of packing and storing our things at the student hostel in London.

On September 22, we caught the afternoon train to Coventry. It had just stopped raining and the roads were still slippery when we left. Our bus driver drove rapidly and skillfully to reach the train station on time. Thanks to him, we just made it. As soon as we settled into our seats, the conductor blew his whistle and the train began to move.

The rhythmic sounds and swaying of the train soon put me to sleep. I slept the whole way until the sudden jerk of the train stopping as we reached our destination awakened me. As we disembarked from the train, Peter Mauger, the head of the Education Department, shook hands with each of us and greeted us in Chinese: "Xia wu hao" (Good afternoon). He had traveled to China several times and knew some phrases in our native tongue. Inside the train station we were greeted by a group from the College of Education composed of several of our teachers, students, and even some of their families and children. The children presented each of us with a small bouquet of flowers picked from their own gardens. We were all surprised and deeply moved by this unexpectedly warm welcome.

We boarded the college bus with this wonderful group of people. Upon our arrival at the college, Peter Mauger made a short welcoming speech. "Ladies and gentlemen," he said, "we are all delighted to receive, for the first time in the college's history, students from China, a country with a long history of civilization, and a country which has achieved tremendous success over the last two decades since the founding of the People's Republic. We are very proud to be the first college of education in this country to welcome Chinese students. I hope you will enjoy your stay in Coventry and have a wonderful experience and a successful year here."

After Mr. Mauger's speech, we expressed our heartfelt thanks for the warm welcome and courtesy extended to us by the teachers, students and their families. A small reception followed where an English afternoon tea was served. After the reception a group of third-year students from the Education Department led us to our residence halls. I was assigned a room in Emscote Hall for the year. We ate supper with the students at the college dining hall. After that they took us on a quick tour of the college.

Coventry College of Education was only 30 years old. It had been built during World War II as an emergency training center for soldiers. After the war it was converted to a teachers' training college for women. In order to meet an increasing demand for teachers, it became coeducational and had developed Art, Music, History, Geography, Sociology and Math-Sciences departments. When I was there, there were about 1,500 students and about 100 teaching staff. It was a small campus and the buildings were compactly laid out. We loved it because it was very convenient for us to go to the library, lecture halls, and dining hall on foot, since none of us had cars or bikes.

Coventry College of Education was incorporated into the University of Warwick in 1978 as the Westwood campus, but it was an excellent teachers' college in the 1970s when I attended. We were told the College had one of the most modern language resource centers in England. We actually made full use of this excellent resource center daily during our studies there. We did a lot of recordings and made many tapes for our future use and resources as teachers.

On our third day in Coventry, the Lord Mayor of Coventry held a reception in our honor at Coventry City Hall. The Lord Mayor and his wife, together with several other officials, shook hands with each of us. The mayor was dressed in a fancy uniform and wore his traditional golden chains of office across his chest and shoulders. He expressed his pleasure in meeting us. Then he asked each of us what cities or provinces in China we were from and how long we were going to stay. All twelve of us answered his inquiries politely, although his strong local accent made it difficult for us to understand all he said. I had also noticed a young man and a young woman sitting in the corner busily jotting down notes. We assumed they were journalists. We were delighted to see our picture with the mayor on the front page of the Coventry local newspaper the next morning.

The Coventry College teaching staff was made up of extremely hospitable, energetic and efficient people. We spent an hour each morning individually working with several English language experts to improve our English. We were also required to attend lectures in different departments. I chose history, sociology, geography, and worked on English reading and composition with Dr. Atkinson.

Ms. Prue, a senior lecturer and an activist in women's studies, was our sociology tutor. From her classes we learned about Britain's social structure, trades and trade unions and the welfare system. She also taught us about the presence of social and economic inequality and racism in British society. We could not understand the huge disparity between the rich and poor classes in Britain. We were shocked to see that there were homeless people in England who lived in parks and slept on park benches. We could not understand how this could happen in a country far richer than China.

From Mr. Douglas Jones and his colleagues in the history department, we learned a brief history of England and the history of other western countries such as Germany, France and the United States. Mr. Jones was head of the History Department and was also an expert on Chinese history. His wife was originally from China, and they had adopted two boys from Hong Kong. One day they invited all 12 Chinese students to visit their home. There we saw a large collection of Chinese antiques including porcelain vases, bowls from the Qing dynasty, carved jade elephants, phoenixes and dragons surrounded by beautiful Chinese landscape paintings, figure paintings and calligraphies. They called it "the China Room." It was like a museum in a private home.

As part of our geography classes, we took short trips to nearby places such as Liverpool, Nottingham, and the Lake District. When we visited Liverpool, I saw the buildings and wharves near the Liverpool waterfront were just like the area where my great aunt lived that I often visited when I was growing up in Shanghai. It made me even more homesick.

One of the trips that I will never forget was to the Lake District. We first went to visit William Wordsworth's cottage, which had been converted to a museum. Entering the cottage, we were given a brief history of the great poet who led a very simple life. Some simple household utensils were displayed, and among the things hanging on the wall there was the certificate of Wordsworth's Royal Poet Laureateship. "That," our guide said as she pointed to the certificate, "Mr. Wordsworth gained by plain living and high thinking. The poet did most of his writing in this house and worked until his death in 1850 at the age of 80."

We stayed in a Youth Hostel overnight. The next morning we climbed Helvellyn Peak which rises 3,300 feet above sea level. The first stage of the climb was difficult. Although the gradient was not steep, the trail was long and arduous because it spiraled around the mountain crest. I was out of breath in just 10 minutes as if I had been running a sprint.

It took us 40 minutes to reach a point 800 feet above sea level, and we had gone only a third of the way to the top. We stopped for a brief rest and then resumed the second stage of our climb. As we climbed higher mists silently swirled out of nowhere, wrapping around us and then vanishing without a trace as quickly as they had come.

Mr. Feely, our geography tutor, warned us of the danger, even the possible loss of life, if we were not extremely careful. Here every step required close attention. Every rock we clutched had to be firm, so we used both our hands and feet to scale the rock face on the last part of our climb. More than two hours after we started our climb, we finally reached the summit. We all felt triumphant to have reached the top. I had never climbed a mountain that high before. The mountain was covered with fog so the view was limited, but I was thrilled to see such beautiful scenery. It was a fun-filled and adventurous day for us all and a welcome break from our studies.

In the English Department, Dr. Atkinson and her colleagues spent their precious time helping us with our English language studies, especially in reading and composition. One day, while listening to Dr. Atkinson reading a poem, I was so enchanted by her lyrical reading skills that I borrowed the poem from her. But when I tried to read it aloud in my room, I was disappointed with my flat intonation and inability to mimic her poetic fluency in English. I admired her skills and began to pay more attention to how people talked and the vocabulary they used in order to be able to speak more naturally and fluently.

Our course at Coventry College of Education ended in June 1975. We had learned so much and established many friendships there, especially with Dr. Atkinson and Peter Mauger. Peter Mauger visited China again in 1981 and came to see me at Shanghai University where I was teaching.

For the last two and a half months, we took summer classes at London University. There were so many choices for summer program! I chose drama and read aloud different characters in several plays. The one I liked most was Pygmalion by George Bernard Shaw. When I was assigned the part of Eliza Doolittle, I listened to the recordings several times before I read aloud in the class. The professor listened, took notes and gave us feedback and instructions. It was a fun summer. We took the tube every morning to go to our classes and to return to our hostel in the afternoon. I felt like I was a Londoner.

When our summer program was over at London University so was our stay in England. My two years in Great Britain had not only improved my English greatly, but had also been a wonderful opportunity to meet and understand the British people, their history, their culture and the whole society. We were grateful for this unique opportunity and to all the teaching staff who had worked tirelessly to train us to be better teachers.

I was looking forward to going back to China and my family and friends who I missed terribly. On the morning of

September 12, we left our student hostel and boarded the train from London to Harwick via Liverpool. We reached Harwick harbor at eleven o'clock. At noon, we boarded a ship bound for Hook, Holland. Then we crossed the English Channel on this beautiful oceangoing ship and arrived in the port city of Hook at six-twenty that evening. At seven o'clock, we caught a Russian train in Hook for the two-day ride to Moscow. When we reached the Russian border, two uniformed Russian customs officers came into our compartment and confiscated all the snacks and fruit we were carrying. By the time we reached Moscow, I was sick and started to cough.

When we arrived in Moscow, we stayed at the Chinese Embassy for two days to rest, and I ate some decent Chinese food. The day after our arrival, we visited Red Square where we stood in line for hours to see Lenin's body. It was preserved in perfect condition. I could even see his mustache very clearly. He looked as if he were sleeping. He was a short, small man just as he had been portrayed in the movies. There were guards at the front gate as well as inside the Kremlin Palace.

After spending two years in England, Moscow seemed colorless and depressing. Most people were dressed in drab colors and wore flat expressions as somber as their clothing. There were lines everywhere in front of stores. We only visited Red Square and spent most of our time resting in the Chinese Embassy.

On September 16, we caught the eight o'clock Chinese evening train to Beijing. It was a six-day trip, but unlike on the Russian train the food was delicious and inexpensive with lots of variety to choose from. They also served excellent wines on the train. I bought a bottle of wine called "Clear Bamboo Leaf

Wine" as a present for my father. Unfortunately, my coughing got worse and I could not enjoy the good food as much as the others. As the distance became shorter and shorter each day, I felt closer and closer to my home and my country.

On the afternoon of September 22, 1975, we finally arrived at the Beijing Train Station. Master Worker Ju's sister, her husband and their two sons were waiting for me at the Beijing Train station. It was wonderful to see their familiar smiling faces greeting me. At last, I was home!

In the past two years, Ju's sister and her husband had not changed a bit, but their two teenage boys were a lot taller and seemed older, especially the elder one who was almost 15. They all said that I had changed a lot, too. I had become thinner and paler. After 10 days of train travel covering over 10,000 miles, I was exhausted. The Ju family wanted me to rest at their home for several days before attempting the remaining 24-hour train ride to Shanghai. But even though I was sick and coughing, I missed my home and my family so much that I insisted on getting home as soon as possible. Ju's sister gave me some Chinese herbal medicine for my cough, so I slept better that night. She asked me to keep some for my train ride home. I only stayed with them one night and left for Shanghai on the train the following day.

9 – Teacher, Wife and Mother
1975-1984

As the train pulled into Shanghai Station on September 25, 1975, I saw my elder brother Youfu, with my younger sister Oufeng waiting on the platform. I was excited and waved to them, but they didn't see me at first. As my train slowly approached the station, they finally saw me and shouted together, "Ta hui lai le! Ta hui lai le! (She is back! She is back!)."

Oufeng had changed a lot. She was 18 when I left, and in the two years of my absence, she had grown taller and stronger. Her arms showed muscles, and she looked like a weightlifter. She had become a truck and fork-lift driver in addition to being the Party Secretary in charge of the brick factory. She carried my two 60-pound suitcases and lifted them both with ease onto the bed of the pick-up truck she had driven to the station. I was amazed. She refused to let Youfu take one of my suitcases, so Youfu just followed along behind us.

Oufeng drove us home in the pick-up truck that she had borrowed from the brick factory. It was a common practice in China for trusted employees who could drive to borrow the company's vehicles on weekends for special occasions. Very few people in China owned private vehicles at that time.

My elder brother Youfu had not changed much since I last saw him three years earlier. He was home from Xinjiang for his annual leave and had coordinated his vacation time in Shanghai with my arrival home in order to see me again. I was happy to see them both. I noticed how confidently Oufeng handled her truck as she carefully negotiated the drive in the heavy afternoon traffic. Driving big trucks was considered a man's job. On the ride home, they filled me in on all the news and updated me on what had happened in China, in Shanghai, in our neighborhood, and to everyone in my family during my two years' absence.

My parents were waiting for us at the front door when we arrived. They both looked older and seemed shorter and smaller to me. Then I saw my youngest sister, Xiao Mei, and my youngest brother, Youfa. They had both grown up so much that I might not have recognized them if I had met them on the street. Their baby faces had disappeared, and they had become young adults. Youfa was 16 and Xiao Mei was 18 now. My second brother, Yougen, was still in the Army; but they told me he would be coming home on leave in a couple of days.

I looked at my home and all the familiar faces around me and I said, "Jing wo, ying wo, bu ru jia li gou wo", which translates to "Gold house, silver house, not as good as your own dog house". A more accurate English meaning is, "East or West, Home is best." But at the same time, I noticed that everything in the house and its contents seemed smaller, older and dingier than they had been before I left. The walls of our house were dark and badly needed new paint. In England I had been exposed to plastered and colorfully painted or papered walls and carpeted floors. At that time my parents' home had a private cold-water tap and gas for the stove. But aside from that, like most Chinese, they didn't have an indoor toilet, hot water or central heating. My youngest sister, Xiao Mei, was now emptying the family chamber-pot at the local dump station, my old job.

The next day I convinced Youfu to paint the walls of our house to make it brighter and cleaner. We went to the store and bought some white paint. Dad wanted to help us and said, "Even though I am now retired, I still have energy and I can still help you." We did not argue with him. He painted the kitchen walls, while my brother and I painted the attic upstairs. Many of our neighbors stopped by our house that day to welcome me home. My parents had kept them informed of my adventures in England over the past two years. My parents were quite proud of me as I was the only one in our neighborhood who was sent abroad to study.

On September 29, I returned to the English Department to report for work and receive my new teaching assignment. Everyone in the English Department was surprised to see how thin I had become. My face had always been round and plump since childhood and my nickname had been "Fan Tong" (meaning round, plump rice container). Since I had not eaten much rice for the last two years, my face had become longer and thinner.

The Dean of our Department told me to take another week off, since October first is the beginning of our week-long National Holiday. This is our Independence Day, which celebrates the end of the civil war and the establishment of Communist China on October 1, 1949. The Dean also told me that I was assigned to teach eight hours of the second-year Intensive Readings as well as two hours of third-year lectures on

Great Britain each week. I would be carrying a 10-hour teaching load, two hours more than the usual eight hours expected of all the teachers.

I was delighted to get my teaching assignment and felt privileged to carry two more hours of teaching. It was also great that I could spend another week with my family. As I was still coughing and wheezing when I talked to the Dean, he ordered me to go to the clinic right away. My old friend Guifang went with me, and the doctor diagnosed me with severe bronchitis. The Chinese herbal medicine I had been taking helped me a lot during my train ride, but my symptoms had increased. The doctor prescribed Western medications and bed rest. I spent the holiday week in bed recovering from my bronchitis.

When I was better I began to prepare my lessons, teaching plans and notes for my lectures. As I embarked on my teaching career, I focused on delivering my lectures in a simple, easy-to-understand, and interesting way. I wanted to give back to my students all the knowledge and wisdom I had learned in order to repay the incredible learning experience I had received.

During the two years I was away, Jianguo had been visiting my family regularly. Even though we did not write to each other often, he seemed to care about me and my family. He was liked by my siblings, and they regarded him as their big brother. Even my grandma liked him very much. She said, "Not many men would wait for their girlfriend for so long. He must love Youfeng very much."

It was true that Jianguo had known me for nearly 10 years and waited for me for nearly six years while I went to college and then to England to study. I felt it was only right to marry him for his care and patience. I was already 27 years old and considered an "old maid" by Chinese standards back then. According to Chinese custom and tradition, I should have had a child by now. I did not know what love really meant, but given all these circumstances, I accepted my responsibility as a dutiful daughter, bowed to what others thought was right and agreed to marry Jianguo.

While I was in England, Jianguo had joined the Communist Party and was promoted to a position as one of the section chiefs of the woolen textile company. He was in charge of the personnel department for over 20 woolen textile factories. It was a very high-level position, especially for such a young man.

Since he was a Party member and I was a teacher, we needed to apply to each other's work units for permission to get married. Communist Party representatives from both of our work units did our background checks, which involved family history, original ancestry, parents' and siblings' work and study records, etc. We passed the investigations. If one of us had not passed the investigation--for example, if one of the parents or siblings had been in jail--the unit leaders or supervisors would have recommended that we not marry. If that happened, couples could still choose to get married against the Party's recommendation; however, to do so would risk any opportunities for future promotions. After we had been notified that we had both passed, we went to Shanghai City Hall at the end of December 1975 and received our marriage license.

On January 1, 1976, we were married. We did not have a big wedding. We both had agreed to save the money we would have spent on a big wedding to buy new furniture for our apartment. There was a small gathering of families and friends. Jianguo's parents asked their son-in-law, who was a chef, to cook a fancy meal at their home.

After the wedding, we both received a three-day paid holiday which was the policy of our work units at that time. We spent our three-day "honeymoon" in Suzhou, a small city about 70 miles north of Shanghai, known as "Venice of the East", "City of Gardens", and "Silk Capital". Suzhou is a place of great beauty with lakes, rivers, ponds, pagodas and unique gardens. Much of the city's transportation was carried out on small boats in a complex canal network.

We visited quite a few gardens with unique designs and landscapes. Even though it was wintertime, the bonsai and non-deciduous trees were green and some were still blooming. The colorful blooming bonsai and green foliage contrasted beautifully with the pale tones of dormant trees and shrubs. We walked a lot in the gardens, along the rivers, by the ponds and ate and shopped at the local markets. These were three of the most relaxing and happy days of my life. We bought a bunch of local specialties and silk scarfs for our family and friends at home.

For the first few months of our married life, we lived with Jianguo's parents and family until I was assigned an apartment by the Shanghai Foreign Languages Institute. Jianguo had two brothers and four sisters. Only the two younger sisters were still living at home when we got married. We had our room upstairs in the attic while his parents and two sisters lived downstairs in two rooms. There was an outdoor kitchen shed a few steps across from the main house where we cooked and ate during the day.

I became pregnant with my daughter in the fall of 1976, about five months after we moved into our new apartment. In early May 1977, two months before the baby was due, Jianguo came home earlier than usual on a Friday afternoon, looking troubled and very depressed. I asked him what was wrong.

"Nothing, really," he said, but he avoided my eyes. I knew there must be something wrong because he had never done this before.

"Look at me. You need to tell me what is going on. I am your wife," I insisted.

"OK, if you really want to know, I was considered a follower of the 'Gang of Four.' I was demoted together with several other young carders from the company. I've been ordered to return to my old factory to work as a mechanic on the night shift starting next Monday," he said.

"What happened? Did you do anything wrong?" I asked.

"No, I just followed the party line and did what I was supposed to do. It's just politics."

"What are you going to do?"

"I have no other choice but to start the night shift as a mechanic next Monday."

"It's all right to return to work at your old factory. I didn't like your involvement in politics anyway," I said, trying to comfort him. He was still miserable. He said he wanted to go out to get some fresh air. I knew he needed some time alone. I watched him walk along the railroad tracks through our windows. It was getting dark. I did not want him to hurt himself or get into some kind of accident, so I went out and followed him. He was a proud man, and I was afraid he might try suicide in order to save face. I was seven months pregnant; our unborn baby and I needed him.

When he saw me following him, he turned towards me. I said, "No matter what happens at work, you always have a home to come to. You are not losing your job. You've just changed your job. It's not really important to me if you are a big shot or not. We are going to be parents soon, so we need to focus on our child and our future."

He seemed to feel a little better after the walk, so we cooked dinner together and talked a little more after dinner. Two weeks before my due date, I returned to my parents' home because the hospital was very close to them, and it would be easy for my mother to take care of me and the baby after my stay at the hospital.

Like my mother, I also experienced water retention and dizzy spells during my pregnancy. My doctor said that I lacked iron and sugar and was anemic. She said I also had Meiniere's disease, which caused the dizzy spells, weakness and nausea. She advised me to rest more and take it easy at work. When I was about five months pregnant, I was released from my teaching duties due to my medical condition. I was assigned to do book translations with a group of retired professors and teachers. This work allowed me to sit most of the day. We were translating a war novel, The Guns of August, written by Barbara W. Tuchman, an American historian. She was awarded the Pulitzer Prize for General Non-Fiction for the publication year of 1963. First, we learned about the background of the First World War, and then we were divided into small groups to translate chapters assigned to each group. We could translate at home or in the office as long as we could hand in one chapter every two weeks. I translated a few more chapters ahead of time because I knew I would have my baby soon.

I was swollen and my feet would not fit into my shoes during my last months of pregnancy. I needed to rest often in a dark, quiet room. The closer I got to my due date, the more swollen I became. On my final checkup, the doctor asked me to stay in the hospital because my due date was only a week away.

I experienced some difficulties during the delivery. But the doctor and nurses were very efficient and prepared with all the latest medical devices. They plugged tubes into my nose and needles into my veins. I was a little nervous, but my mother had successfully delivered her last baby Youfa in the same hospital 18 years before. After almost 10 hours of labor, as I became weaker, the doctor decided to use forceps to help with the baby's head position. Finally, she asked me for the last big push, and I gave it my all. A few minutes later I had a healthy, beautiful little girl in my arms. It was the evening of July 10, 1977.

After my daughter was born, I stayed in the hospital for a few more days. During those days, I rested and did a lot of thinking. I found that I looked at the world differently now that I had become a mother. I had been transformed from a girl just by delivering my daughter. I appreciated my family and my life even more. When I left the hospital with my newborn baby, my husband and my mother came to pick us up in a taxi that waited at the hospital entrance and took me straight to my parents' home.

Mother took care of me and the baby, just like my grandma used to do. My daughter was tiny; she weighed only six pounds, but her features and her little hands and feet were perfect, just like a little angel. I later gave her the English name,

Angel. My four-year-old niece (my elder brother's first child) was also living with my parents at that time. She counted the baby's ten toes and ten fingers to be sure they were all there.

It was a very hot and humid summer and we were always glad to get the ocean breeze during the summer months. We all hoped for more winds and waves from the East China Sea to alleviate the heat. In the heavy heat one evening, my family and I sat around the baby to discuss what to name her. We said Chinese names out loud as we thought of them. The baby was sleeping in her cradle and did not respond in any way until my mother, thinking of the sea breeze and waves, said "Xiao Bo", and the baby murmured or grunted. So, her Chinese name became "Xiao Bo" (Little Wave.) or

I should have received the usual 56-day maternity leave with pay, but it was the annual summer holiday for all teachers in China, so as soon as the summer vacation was over, my maternity leave also ended. I went back to work on the first day of the fall semester while my daughter started her nursery on the same day when she was barely two months old.

Now, I had suddenly added the role of a mother to my original roles as a teacher and a wife. Attempting to fulfill these roles with no help from my still-depressed husband soon left me exhausted and tired most of the time. I was sad and didn't know what to do. Xiao Bo and I needed his help, but he was not there for us. I went to work early in the mornings, fed the baby three to four times a day between my classes (luckily it was only a 10 to 15 minute walk each way from the English Department to the nursery), and picked her up after work. When I got home, I had to do all the cooking and washing for my family of three. After dinner, I prepared my lessons and graded papers until everything was ready for the next day. The only things my husband ever did were washing dishes and occasional cooking--if he was in a good mood.

During the first five years of our marriage, both of us worked hard to save money and purchase all the things we thought a modern family needed (a color TV, a washing machine, a refrigerator, and even a piano for our daughter to learn to play). Half of the time I felt satisfied, because I had a good job, a nice apartment, brand-new furniture, modern appliances, and most importantly, a lovely daughter. I had a better lifestyle than that of my parents' and my grandparents' generations. But half of the time I was sad because I had no partner helping. I had to carry the heavy load--a mountain on my back--no matter how exhausted I was.

The one thing that pushed me through these years was watching my daughter grow from a baby into a smart, inquisitive girl. One Sunday afternoon when Xiao Bo was about six, I was mopping the floor and asked Xiao Bo to sit on her bed so that I could clean the whole floor fast. So she climbed onto her bed and began to read her Little Friends, the children's magazine that she loved. While I was mopping the dust under her bed, my husband finally came into the room to help me. He smelled of cigarettes. He started to dust the table and the piano, then suddenly he grabbed the paintings and artworks Xiao Bo had made at school, which I had displayed on the walls and on our piano.

"We need to make our apartment shipshape and we don't need to keep all this stuff around," he said. He even grabbed a stack of Xiao Bo's books and magazines from the last shelf of the bookcase, "We can recycle these at the collection station and get some money back."

Xiao Bo was mad at her father but she asked calmly, "Comrade Baba, how many people do we have in our family?" Xiao Bo had learned from adults to use "Comrade" when talking about serious matters.

"Three," her father answered.

"So, if I am one of the three, why are you getting rid of my stuff without asking me?"

"Oh, I thought you had already read them."

"But I like to read them again and again!" Xiao Bo raised her voice at her father this time. I joined the conversation; we finally reached an agreement that Xiao Bo could keep all her books and magazines, two pieces of her artwork on the piano, and two of her paintings on the wall.

That was typical of my husband, insensitive to our six-year-old daughter's education and needs and our family's wellbeing.

Ever since my husband's demotion in the company, he had changed into a different person. He increased his smoking and drinking. He refused to talk to anyone, even though I tried to talk to him. I knew he felt he had "lost face" and felt humiliated when he lost his high position at the company, but he took it too personally. It was a major blow to his ego, and he never recovered.

I tried to convince him it was better not to be involved in politics and to have a stress-free job at the factory. I did not mind us being "small potatoes" and living a simple life. I asked him to focus on the most important things in our life—our family and our daughter. I also encouraged him to do something to better himself. One day I said, "Look at your friend Xiao Yang. He was a follower of the 'gang of four' and was demoted, just like you. But he went back to college to major in mechanical engineering. Why don't you go ahead and do the same?"

"I am not as smart as Xiao Yang. Plus, I am already married with a kid and Xiao Yang is not. He thinks he needs to have a college degree to impress his girlfriend."

His response angered me. "So you don't think you need to do anything to improve yourself in order to impress your wife and your daughter? As a matter of fact, you are smarter than Xiao Yang. You are just lazy."

I didn't know how to help him. I was too tired to do anything other than maintain my duties as a mother, a teacher, a wife, and the oldest daughter of my parents. I tried to focus my energy on raising our daughter and being a good teacher like my mentors, Mrs. Zheng, Miss Sun, Miss Benze, and Dr. Atkinson. I threw myself into my work and took care of our daughter. That was all I had energy for.

As my former teachers had modeled for me, I always tried to do what I could for my students. On one occasion, one of my evening school students became ill and had been admitted to the Shanghai Military Hospital in the city suburbs. She was a good student and always completed her work conscientiously and on time. Her illness prevented her from taking the final written, oral and listening examinations for my classes. If she missed this final, she would have had to repeat the whole semester the following year. Considering her future and her unique situation, I decided to make special arrangements with the English Department and the hospital to give her the examinations in her hospital bed. This also required special arrangements with a friend to pick up my daughter from kindergarten.

On the day of the examination, after dropping my daughter off at the kindergarten, I caught a noon bus and transferred to two more buses to reach the hospital all the way across town. I carried with me a heavy tape recorder and all the testing materials. The examination took about two hours. My student was very well prepared, or it could have taken longer.

On my way home, I hit heavy traffic. It took me about three hours to get back to my office and put my materials away. The whole day had passed by the time I finally picked up my daughter at my friend's place. But it was worth the effort, for it saved my student six months or more to not have to repeat the class. She graduated on time, and I was very proud and happy for her. This was over 30 years ago, but I am still glad that I was able to make a little difference in my student's future career.

Striving to be a good teacher to my students and a good mother to my daughter propelled me to get up every morning and kept going. Fortunately, during that period I had a dear friend and colleague who supported me. She shared my first name, Phoenix. She was a peasant student and had been invited to join the English faculty after graduation as I had. She was one of the top students in her graduating class and had been trained by our phonetic expert in the English Department.

I used to stop at Phoenix's home before picking up my daughter from kindergarten. After chatting with her, I always went home feeling much better. Phoenix and I would read the same English novels and talk about the authors, their writings, and the characters in the books. We secretly read Lady Chatterley's Lover by D.H. Lawrence and discussed characters in the book. Actually, we learned a lot about love and sex from our readings. We knew very little, because sex was never openly discussed in China.

When my daughter was six and started school, I had more time to myself to think. I began to question myself and my life more seriously. I asked myself, "Is this the kind of life I dreamed of? Am I happy with my marriage? Can I leave my husband and daughter?" My answer to all of these questions was, "No!"

I could not leave my daughter. She was too young and I loved her too much. But at the same time, I suffered daily because I could not leave my failed marriage. My husband and I no longer even talked to each other or did things together. We ceased being intimate in any way as we drifted further apart over the years. I became more and more exhausted because he did not help me at all. He lived a separate life from us. Sometimes he did not even come home for dinner or to sleep. My daughter was growing up essentially without a father.

Every evening after dinner, Xiao Bo would do her homework and then practice her piano while I corrected my students' papers and prepared my lessons. If my husband was at home, he would go out to smoke and visit our neighbors.

By bedtime, I was totally exhausted and always fell asleep as soon as my head hit the pillow. Several times my husband sexually assaulted me while I was in a deep sleep. At the time I did not realize this was rape, but I felt I had been violated. This was what I wrote in my diary of that traumatic experience more than 30 years ago:

"I believe no women in the world nowadays are supposed to suffer the pain and tortures like mine from their husbands. Every day, I take my daughter to school early in the morning, teach during the day and pick up my daughter on my way back home. Then I have to cook dinner, take care of the household, grade papers, and prepare my lesson plans in the evening. At the end of the day, I can hardly keep my eyes open. No sooner have I closed my eyes than I fall into a deep sleep. But during my deep sleep, I have been disturbed several times and gone through an awful experience which can only be sensed, not explained. It's like a terrible earthquake! I was in the seismic center, falling into a pitch dark hell, sinking deeper and deeper. I knew I was being violated subconsciously, but I could do nothing. I had no control. I was in a state between waking and sleep. I knew I needed to wake up to stop it, but I just could not wake up. I fell back into the nightmare again and again...

"When I finally gathered up all my strength and did wake up, I screamed at him. He seemed asleep, saying he did not know what he was doing. I was so naive the first time that I actually believed him. I told him what an awful time I just had, and that I'd rather die than be violated like that. I begged him to please wake me up if he needed sex next time. I was his wife after all. He promised that he would not violate me again. But in fact, he repeated this kind of act several more times in the next year before I finally kicked him out of our bed."

One time when this had happened, Xiao Bo was awakened by my weeping and screaming. She did not know what had happened to her mother, but she was scared and began crying, too. After that, my husband and I slept separately. I slept with my daughter in our big bed. He slept in my daughter's bed in the next room. He accepted this arrangement because he knew he was wrong. To protect my daughter, I didn't tell her what happened until she was much older.

How I loathed this man who was my husband! I could not understand how he had become so vulgar and insensitive. I had never hated anyone in my life, but I hated him after those experiences. I was too ashamed to tell anyone about it, not even my mother, so writing it in my diary was the only way I had to deal with it. There was no place I could go to ask for help. In China this was not supposed to happen in a "good" marriage, but if it did, it was considered your fault and your problem. We were taught to accept our fate—to "swallow" it.

I only once consulted my close friend Phoenix. She advised me to talk to a doctor to inquire what was wrong with my husband. I never did because I could not and did not know how to express it out loud. I just had to endure or leave the marriage, but I couldn't leave the marriage; I had my daughter to consider.

By the time my daughter was seven or eight years old, my husband had become a total stranger to us. He was addicted to playing Mahjong and gambling with his friends at work. Sometimes he did not even go to work and stayed away from home for days at a time. I never knew what he was doing or where he was going because he began to lie to me. Once he told me that he was sick and staying with his parents, but when I called his parents, they told me they did not know where he was. I finally made up my mind to leave this failed marriage. There was no shelter of any kind for women and children in China, so I approached my mother for assistance.

"Mama, I need to leave my husband. Can I return home with my daughter to live with you?" I asked. Of course, I couldn't tell my mother about being sexually abused by my husband because we didn't talk about such things. It was too embarrassing to tell my parents. Mother was concerned for me, but responded in the traditional way, "You are my oldest daughter. I expect you to do the right thing. We do not want people to gossip behind our backs." She was worried about the public scandal and "loss of face" a divorce would bring.

At that time, divorce was not common and was frowned upon; it was considered a failure. My mother knew people would gossip and then the whole family would lose face.

"Mama, why should we care about what other people say?" I asked.

Mother answered with an old Chinese proverb, "There is an old saying: 'Jia ji sui ji, jia gou sui gou' (marry a chicken and share the coop, marry a dog and share the kennel). You are the oldest sister. You are supposed to set a good example to all your younger brothers and sisters."

Even had I been able to tell her about the sexual abuses by my husband, she would not have replied differently. No matter what happened or how badly I felt, it was unthinkable for me to talk about sexual matters with my mother, and she could not have people gossip behind our backs.

I tried hard to hold back my tears. For the first time, my mother did not know what to do to help me. I was devastated, but I was determined to be a strong woman and carry on as I had always been taught to do. My mother expected me to maintain the family honor and to be a dutiful daughter, mother and wife. So that was what I did for five more years.

During those painful, difficult years, I felt like a bird in a cage that could never escape. I knew I needed to do something to change my life and my daughter's life for the better. But what could I do? How should I do it? I was trapped in a failed marriage. I remember many sleepless nights pacing on my small balcony, deep in thought and struggling for a solution. But I could not find any. I remained stuck, but all the while I was still trying very hard to provide my daughter a normal life.

Every Sunday morning, I took Xiao Bo to her piano teacher, who was a professor at the Shanghai Conservatory of Music. We had to take two buses to get to her apartment on Huaihai Road. After a half-hour piano lesson, we continued on our way to my parents' house. This was the best part of Xiao Bo's Sundays, when she could spend time with Grandma and Grandpa and play with her cousins. We four siblings in Shanghai visited each other, cooked food together and gave our parents a break from their daily routine.

My daughter tells me that these Sunday visits remain some of her fondest childhood memories. They are also my best memories from that darkest period in my life. They were the only respite in my six-day work routine. They allowed me to survive emotionally through those painful years.

When I was writing this chapter, I didn't know that just writing about it would bring up so much old pain and bad memories. I couldn't sleep for several days. I thought I was healed after more than 30 years, but I wasn't. I was a complete emotional wreck for two weeks. With the help of my current husband and my daughter, I was able to face this deeply-buried issue. I took their advice and went to see a counselor for a few sessions before I could continue writing this book.

I learned from my counselor that I may never be completely healed, but I have learned to let it go and embrace my new life with gratitude and contentment. I also learned from my own research that the most misunderstood area of sexual assault is marital rape. The psychological trauma in marital rape is especially profound because the woman's trust is shattered regarding the individual whom she has the most need to trust. Studies have found that even six months after the rape, the majority of victims still experience "core distress". Fifteen to 30 months after the rape, more than 40 percent of women still suffer sexual dysfunction, fear and depression. Three years after the rape, a variety of psychological symptoms persist, leading researchers to believe that many victims never recover completely. My distress in writing about this traumatic experience more than 30 years after it occurred shows me that resolution of this kind of trauma is very difficult and seldom final.

In December 2015 the Chinese government passed the country's first landmark bill against domestic violence. A new law that came into effect in March 2016, finally recognized spousal abuse as an offense in its own right. But activists say that the law has not been implemented effectively enough. U.N. Women has been trying to raise the awareness of women's rights and provide legal advocacy, while also working with police and the legal system to help women access the services available to them. I applaud the passing of these bills in China even though they were three decades too late to help me. I am happy to see more women in China will be protected by the law, and they will have access to services which had never existed before.

During that darkest period of my life without support from my family and friends (except Phoenix's advice to talk to a doctor), I thought about committing suicide by turning on the gas in the kitchen. Whenever this crazy idea came up, I thought of my daughter, my parents, and all my students. What would happen to my seven-year-old daughter if I died? How would it affect my aging parents, my siblings, my students and all my friends? I realized that I could never do anything like that! I was only 35 years old. I had a long way to go, and I had too many responsibilities towards too many people.

At that time, I never told anyone of my suicidal thoughts, but some of my close friends noticed my distress and were very concerned. Some of my friends and students wrote to me from America where they had gone to study. One of my former students Yaoyao had written saying, "Teacher Shen, you are like a candle lighting other people's roads while burning yourself down. Why don't you come to America as a graduate student too? You can bring your daughter and your parents to America once you get your degree and find a job. A lot of people are doing that."

Yaoyao was right. I had helped quite a few students prepare for their TOEFL and GRE exams and visa interviews to achieve this very thing. I had never thought of myself as a graduate student in America before, but I certainly knew how to become one. I decided to take his advice. There was no reason why I couldn't do what some of my friends and students had already done. I decided to go to America as a graduate student to pursue a higher degree. I could eventually bring my daughter and my parents to America for a better life and escape my failed marriage. If I could not get any help in China, I could always leave. Now, I finally had a plan.

10 – My Five-Year Plan
1984-1989

The upper age limit for graduate studies in China was set at 35. I was already 36 in 1984 when I began thinking about pursuing graduate studies in America, which gave me an acceptable reason to request further studies in America from the English Department. I did not know how long the request would take or whether I would be successful or not. Based on my friends' experiences, some took a couple of years and others took four to five years depending on their individual situations. Since I didn't have any relatives in America, only a few good friends, I gave myself five years to accomplish my plan.

During the first two years of my five-year plan, I spent at least several hours every week browsing through the American university catalogues that our library had on the shelves. I wrote down the names and addresses of the universities in which I was interested, along with the names of department heads or contact persons. I also read all the application requirements, choices of majors, and any other relevant information for foreign students. My friends recommended some books I could borrow from the library, and I read as much as I could about American history, culture, and the people of this fascinating country with great opportunity.

In 1986 I began the actual process of applying to American universities for graduate studies. My friend and former classmate Jade was living in New York City with her husband. Her husband worked as a translator for the Chinese delegation to the United Nations. When they came to visit me during their vacation in the summer of 1987, they had to wait for me for two hours until I finished my evening classes. They spent some time talking with my daughter while waiting for me. Seeing that my daughter was often home alone while I taught evening classes, they were concerned about her well-being as well. When they found out about the state of my marriage, they felt deeply troubled and sorry for us. When I told them I was in the process of applying to American graduate schools, they spontaneously offered to help me in any way they could. I appreciated their support and promised that I would let them know when I needed their help.

My former professor in England, Dr. Atkinson, was also happy to sponsor me and write letters of reference on my behalf. With the assurances and support of my former professor and these good friends, I began the intricate application process. I made a list of the major steps it would take for me to reach my goal. They were as follows:

1. Narrow down a list of American universities and names of department heads to which I would apply.
2. Send letters of inquiry to five of these universities requesting application forms for admission, financial support forms, and other forms to the master's level programs in English, education, and related majors.

3. Register for the TOEFL (Test of English as a Foreign Language) in Shanghai, held twice yearly, and prepare for and take the examination.

4. Select the top three universities, complete the application forms and submit fees, which May and her husband would send directly to the universities for me.

5. Obtain my Chinese and British college transcripts, translate the Chinese transcripts into English and certify the translations. Ask each school to send the transcripts directly to the universities I would be applying to.

6. Request Dr. Atkinson to be my sponsor and complete the sponsor section of the application forms.

7. Obtain three letters of reference from my professors and mentors familiar with my academic performance and teaching skills.

8. Apply for a passport as soon as I receive the I-20 Foreign Student Status letter from an American university. Obtain my birth certificate and translate it into English, along with other necessary documents.

9. Get vaccinations and a physical examination at the Shanghai Health Department. Obtain government permission to leave China for educational purposes.

10. Get all documentation ready and go to the American Consulate for a visa application interview.

During this whole five-year process, unexpected events occurred along the way. Most notably, my plans were interrupted by the Tiananmen Square protests of 1989. In May1989 a student-led hunger strike gained momentum and support from all walks of life in China. Thousands of students marched through Tiananmen Square carrying banners, chanting slogans and singing songs that called for a more democratic political atmosphere. The government's response to the demonstrations and to the students was painfully slow and harsh. Officials who showed any sympathy towards the students were purged. Several of the demonstration leaders were arrested. A propaganda campaign was directed at the marching students, declaring that they sought to "create chaos under the heavens".

Many of my own students had left their classrooms and gone to the People's Square in Shanghai to demonstrate in support of the Beijing students at Tiananmen Square. Staring at their empty seats and thinking about the future of our country affected me deeply. One afternoon when I got home, I could not control myself and wept. Just then, my 11-year-old daughter returned home from school and saw my tears. She came to me quietly and asked me in a worried voice, "What is wrong, Mama?"

All I could think about when I looked at her sweet, soft face was the fear that she might be amongst the demonstrating students one day, sacrificing her life in the vain hope of reaching an unhearing government. I hugged her tightly and said, "I'm fine. I am just worried about the students in Tiananmen Square. I hope our government will do the right thing soon before they lose their young lives during the hunger strike."

Like any typical 11-year-old, she replied excitedly, "Mama, I tell you, all my classmates want to support the big brothers and sisters in Tiananmen Square."

"I know, Xiao Bo, but you are too young to understand. Just go to school and come home as soon as school's over. Don't do anything or say anything without talking to me first," I warned her with trepidation and a sense of foreboding.

As the days went by, the situation in Beijing became more and more tense. Finally on June 3, 1989, the government did something that shocked all of China and the entire world. Overnight everything changed. Military units from rural parts of China entered Beijing and killed hundreds, and by some reports, thousands of people in Tiananmen Square.

The local Beijing-based military units had refused to fire on their own people. The morning after the massacre, the announcer on Radio Beijing's English-language service somberly began his news report: "Remember June 3, 1989. A most tragic event happened in the Chinese capital, Beijing. Thousands of unarmed people, most of them innocent civilians, were killed by fully-armed soldiers who forced their way into Beijing... The soldiers were riding in armored vehicles and used machine guns against thousands of unarmed local residents and students who tried to block their way... Radio Beijing deeply mourns those who died in this tragic incident and appeals to all its listeners to join our protest against this gross violation of human rights and this most barbarous suppression of our people."

That same day, staff members at the People's Daily managed to print a brief report that alluded to the enormous number of civilian casualties resulting from the army's rampage. They acknowledged that "martial-law troops have already stormed Tiananmen square". But just a few days later, papers had become virtually devoid of any news about the massacre or the military crackdown by the government.

In Shanghai, we watched and waited with fear. Suddenly, the familiar, friendly faces and voices of the TV news announcers and radio commentators were replaced by completely new faces and new voices, voicing strong opposition to the student hunger strike. But we all knew what had really happened.

In the ensuing days, the true news of what had happened drifted to us piece-by-piece by word of mouth from friends abroad and at home. We all mourned. I mourned for all the young lives lost, for all the grieving parents and for my country. The country I loved, but which I could no longer understand. I mourned for my powerlessness, for my inability to help my people and protect my loved ones. After this senseless and terrible tragedy, I felt a deep despair over what had happened in my country. I was filled with an urgency to continue my plans to leave China and to find a way to bring my parents and especially my daughter to America.

In early May of 1989, I received my I-20 foreign student status letter from the University of Cincinnati, Ohio. I was offered a $14,000 annual scholarship for my graduate studies in the College of Education. I accepted the offer right away. But during the demonstrations, the U.S. Consulate in Shanghai closed its doors for about two months. I waited anxiously for the doors to reopen so I could obtain my visa to America. This was the last hurdle before I could leave China.

At the same time, I was being pressured by my English Department at Shanghai University to stay. I needed their permission to leave my teaching position for further studies in America. I promised the Dean of the English Department that I would return to teach as soon as I received my degree. But in my heart, I knew I would not come back as long as China remained unchanged politically. When I finally got approval from Shanghai University, I had to apply to the Shanghai Education Bureau for Higher Learning. After checking my records and all the paper work, the Shanghai Education Bureau for Higher Learning also wanted to stop me from leaving.

One of the officers said, "We don't understand why your university agreed to let you leave. You have studied in England, and we can surely use you in our department."

"I didn't get my graduate degree in England. The English Department did not agree to let me go at first, but I promised I would return to teach for the university in two years."

The officer was not convinced and said, "We cannot approve your application without further investigation. We will let you know once we have made a decision." I was let down, but I could do nothing except wait. I was not going to give up. Failure was not an option. I rode my bike to the Educational Bureau on Huaihai Road to check my status every day, even when it was 100 degrees Fahrenheit. I sat in their waiting room with a book, patiently awaiting their decision. Sometimes I requested to talk to the director or anyone who was in charge. That was how I spent the last two weeks of July, my last summer vacation in Shanghai.

My concerned friends suggested that I should try to go through the "back door" and bribe the director of that department. I always hated people who bribed Party officials to get what they wanted. I didn't know how to bribe anyone. Should I take the bribe to the director's home, his office, or some mutually agreed place? I didn't even know if he would accept a bribe.

Since I couldn't possibly bribe anyone and didn't know how, I tried to find some other way. I have often heard that "where there's a will, there's a way". I decided to gather a few good friends for their advice. One of my friends' mother had been a former boss of the current secretary to the Mayor of Shanghai, Mr. Zhu Rongji. She had personally talked to Zhu's secretary about my case. The Mayor's secretary said the Education Bureau had no right to stop anyone from pursuing further education. After reporting my case to Mr. Zhu, the Mayor's office issued a letter allowing me to leave China for further studies. My persistence and connections had paid off in the end.

As soon as I received the letter of approval, I went to the Police Department to apply for a passport. This would normally have taken about a month, but I got my passport within two weeks because I found another connection with the Police Department through a family friend whose son had been my student. When the U.S. Consulate in Shanghai opened its doors again in August, I had all my required paperwork and was ready to apply for my visa to America.

Every morning, there were hundreds of people lined up waiting in front of the American Consulate to try their luck at leaving China. Each day only two or three people were successful in obtaining U.S. visas. It was a hot day in August 1989 when I applied for my visa. There was already a long line in front of the American Consulate when I arrived at seven o'clock. Some people told me that the line usually started around five or five-thirty and many had been standing there for almost two hours. When the Consulate opened its doors at eight-thirty, there were already hundreds of people in line. My little sister Xiao Mei and I stood in that line for more three hours in the hot sun.

When it was my turn to be interviewed, it took me only about ten minutes. The American officer in the student visa section was a young man in his late 20s. He looked through my papers and asked me the usual questions.

"Why do you want to go to America?"

"To study for my Master's degree," I replied.

"How are you going to pay for your education?"

"I have been offered a scholarship by the University of Cincinnati. My former Professor, Dr. Atkinson is my sponsor."

After the officer double-checked the I-20 form with a University Graduate Scholarship of $14,000 a year and the $7,000 in savings in the Bank of China under my name, he signed and stamped "Approved" right in front of me. My friends, YaoYao, Jade and her husband had opened an account with the Bank of China in New York City and deposited $7000 of their own money under my name for me to use when I went to America. I had never asked for it, but they wanted me to have it and told me not to worry about returning the money until I had finished my studies and got a job. Because of my professor and my friends' trust in me and their generous support, I had finally succeeded.

My little sister waited for me outside the gates of the U.S. Consulate while I went inside to get my visa. She told me that I was only the second person who had come out with a smiling face that morning. It was almost noon so we hurried back to her apartment to eat lunch. She had already prepared our lunch the day before. She brought out some cold chicken in Shaoxing wine sauce (my favorite summer dish), pickled cucumber and a fruit salad from her refrigerator, and we both sat down to a delightful lunch.

I was relieved, but there was still a lot of work to do before I could leave China. We discussed what I needed to do and what she could do for me before I left. Then we wrote down another list:

1. Report my U.S. Visa status to the head of the English Department at Shanghai University and write a letter of intention promising that I would return as soon as I earned my degree.

2. Return all the books I had borrowed from different libraries.

3. Go to the Health Department and get shots. (My sister offered to go with me since it was far from the city, and she wanted to give me some support.)

4. Go to the Police Department and get a clearance that I was not involved in the current student movement. I was glad I had stayed out of all politics as my father had advised us so many times.

5. Go to the main office of Bank of China and convert the regulated amount of Chinese yuan into U.S. dollars.

Everything went as planned until I went to the Health Department. While I was having my physical, the doctor found that I had a spot on my lung. He asked me if I'd had tuberculosis in my lungs in the past. I replied in the negative. He said he couldn't give me a pass if I didn't clear this up. Xiao Mei and I were both shocked. I had worked so hard to get this far; I couldn't believe I would be stopped now.

Suddenly, Xiao Mei remembered something and said, "Jie Jie, you had some kind of skin problem when you were young. Was it a tuberculosis skin problem?"

"Oh yes, it was. But I was healed a long time ago," I said. The doctor checked the X-Ray again and said, "This is an old spot, and it is not active, so I can let you pass." We were both relieved when we heard this. I was so stressed out by the whole process that I wasn't thinking properly. If it hadn't been for my little sister Xiao Mei, who was so quick and smart, I might not have made it over this last hurdle.

I was blessed with such a caring family. Everyone in my family supported my aspirations, but it was my youngest sister who came to my rescue when I needed it the most.

Xiao Mei was having marital problems with her husband at about the same time I was. We understood each other intuitively even though we didn't talk about such matters. Since we could not get any support from our parents or other siblings in connection with our marital problems, we bonded in ways that no one else could understand. My escape plan encouraged her because she knew I would eventually help her, too.

When I finally got my visa, with the health and political clearances, I was elated. I had finally made it! Soon I would be flying to America through the vast, open sky.

At the same time, I was also very sad to leave my country, my family, and especially my 12-year-old daughter. I couldn't take Xiao Bo with me. Xiao Bo understood the situation surprisingly well. She said, "Mama, I know why you have to leave us."

"Tell me what you know, Xiao Bo."

"You want to have a better life for you and for me. You want to take Grandma and Grandpa with us. You don't want me to be killed like those big brothers and sisters at the Tiananmen Square."

"How do you know so much?"

"You were talking to my Little Aunt. You are going to America fifty percent for you and fifty percent for me. I am already 12 years old. I understand."

I was heartbroken to hear her say this, but it was true. I was very proud of her maturity at such a young age. I knew that my family would take good care of her while I was away and that she would be safe. My husband had also finally agreed to divorce me once I was out of China. He didn't want a divorce while I was in China because he didn't want to "lose face." Leaving him was a great relief. But leaving my daughter behind was the hardest thing I had ever done. I just hoped I would be able to make it up to her in the future.

On September 20, 1989, Shanghai University sent a van to my apartment to pick me and my family up and take us to the airport. Two of my colleagues from the English Department also came to see me off. There were many tears at the airport. I wished my parents could have been there, but they always stayed behind to weep together at home when one of us left. They were old-fashioned and felt that weeping in public would be too embarrassing. They loved us all and could not bear to see us leave them and fly away.

Eleven hours after take-off, I saw San Francisco shimmering white and orange in the early morning sunlight far below. My heart was beating faster and faster as the plane approached San Francisco International Airport. The moment the plane touched down on American soil, I tried to deplane as quickly as I could. When I finally managed to get off the plane, my first act was to kneel down and kiss the ground. I wondered as I stood up, tears running down my cheeks, how many countless others had done this before me and how many more would do the same after me. I felt like a bird that had just been released from its cage, ready to fly into the unknown world.

Youfeng Shen

Epilogue

At the time I left China, my mother was 67 and my dad was already 79. I was afraid I might not be able to see my father again. I hoped he would not pass away during the two years I was in America getting my degree. I was determined to bring my parents and my daughter to America as soon as I finished my graduate studies and found a job.

I didn't know it at the time, but this would be the last time I would ever see my mother. She died unexpectedly eight months after I left. Her death was the second-hardest thing ever to happen to me in my life. I did see my father again, when I returned to China on a visit. But I was never able to show him America either.

I knew deep down in my heart that my parents loved me and were very proud of me, even though they didn't say it aloud. I wish I could have shown them America because I got here because of them. They had made me who I was, had taught me to be strong, and, more importantly, they had taught me to value the importance of an education for a woman. Their unconditional love allowed me to believe in my intrinsic worth and gave me the courage to change my life.

Both my daughter and I have each carved out successful lives in America since we were reunited in 1992, three years after my departure. There were many struggles, hard work and tears, as well as joys and successes. My life and struggles in America will be told at another time and in another story.

I have achieved all the goals I had set for myself. I did not know that my decision to immigrate to America would eventually free me of the mountain I had carried on my back for so long, but that's what came to pass. I am now as free as a bird and happy with my life.

Afterword

I would like to close my story with the words of the famous American writer, Helen Adams Keller: "Life is either a daring adventure or nothing."

Helen Keller's life was a spectacular inspiration for all mankind, but especially for women and people with disabilities. I admire and identify with both her and her teacher, Annie Sullivan. I cannot possibly compare my life to theirs. However, I may humbly say that my life has been full and somewhat daring for a Chinese woman. In no small part this has been due to the inspiration I have drawn from these two great American women, my mentors and others I admire.

We are the authors of our own lives and we live with what we create.

About the Author

Youfeng Shen taught ESL (English as a Second Language) and Chinese for 25 years in China and in the U.S. After graduating from Shanghai Foreign Languages Institute in 1973, she became a teaching assistant until she was chosen by the Chinese government to pursue advanced studies in English in Great Britain for two years.

Upon completion of her studies in England, she returned to China, where she taught English at Shanghai Foreign Languages Institute and Shanghai University for the next fourteen years. In 1989, Ms. Shen was offered a graduate scholarship from the University of Cincinnati, where she received her Master's in education degree in 1992. She taught ESL and Chinese language at Western Nevada Community College and the University of Nevada, Reno.

While teaching at Shanghai University, she co-authored English Correspondence & Communication, a textbook used by Chinese universities and colleges. She also translated chapters of the novel The Guns of August from English to Chinese. She has written cross-cultural articles for The World Journal and Sing Tao Daily.

Ms. Shen drinks cups of green tea all day long and enjoys occasional bubble tea with her daughter and grandson when they are around.

Youfeng Shen

Printed in Great Britain
by Amazon